Minnesota
Times & Tastes

Governor Arne and First Lady Susan Carlson

Minnesota Times & Tastes

Recipes & Menus
Seasoned with History
from the
Minnesota Governor's
Residence

edited by
Jean Steiner

The 1006 Summit Avenue Society is a non-profit organization established in 1982 to help support the Minnesota Governor's Residence. Membership in the society is open to the public.

For information on where to get copies of *Minnesota Times & Tastes,* call the Governor's Residence at (612) 297-2161, or write to:

> *Minnesota Times & Tastes,*
> The Governor's Residence,
> 1006 Summit Avenue,
> St. Paul, Minnesota 55105

Library of Congress Number: 93-086792
ISBN Number: 0-9606852-1-9
Manufacturer's Number: 781474

Copyright © 1993
The 1006 Summit Avenue Society
St. Paul, Minnesota 55105
First Edition, All Rights Reserved.

Printed in the United States of America on recycled paper
by Gopher State Litho, 3232 East 40th Street, Minneapolis, MN 55406.

Design and desktop publishing by Barbara Ladd, St. Paul, Minnesota

Price $24.95 plus tax
All proceeds from sale of the book go toward maintenance and refurbishing of the Minnesota Governor's Residence

My heartfelt thanks to The 1006 Summit Avenue Society for sponsoring this cookbook project as a fundraiser for the residence; to the many who gave their time and talents and made the project a success; to all the people for whom Minnesota is home, who live near the lakes and wooded areas, in the green valleys and farmlands, in the cities and small towns of this beautiful state; and especially to the children on whom its future depends.

— *Susan Carlson*

Contents

Preface

This book salutes Olivia Irvine Dodge, who was born at 1006 Summit Avenue and spent her childhood there, and, who with her sister, gave the house to the State of Minnesota as a Governor's Residence, and who continues her support of the residence.

It honors, too, the first ladies of Minnesota who contributed to the stewardship of the house, who lived there and made it function as a home and an official state house during major renovation and constant, ongoing restoration.

They applied their talents and gave generously of their efforts to preserve and enhance the history the house embodies. They are the unsung heroines in the success of the house as a state ceremonial building.

The book is one of First Lady Susan Carlson's fundraising projects for the residence, in cooperation with the 1006 Summit Avenue Society. She wanted a "Minnesota book," and so the most recognizable Minnesota symbol, the loon, appears on its pages.

The bird's clear call is a sound of home in the land of 10,000 lakes, where it summons Minnesotans and visitors to the tranquility of blue skies and waters, farmlands, and wooded countryside that make Minnesota "L'Etoile du Nord" (The Star of the North).

The Carlsons welcome guests to the fundraising 80th birthday celebration for the residence in 1991.

Hospitality

at the

Governor's Residence

"It takes
a heap o' livin'
t' make a house a home."

Edgar Albert Guest

Through the years, the grand old house at 1006 Summit Avenue has welcomed seven families, adapted to their lifestyles, and changed with the times. In the early 1900s, the Horace Irvines, who built the house, filled it with gracious living — servants to help with the children, late-evening garden parties, and holiday celebrations rich in family tradition.

For 52 years, the house served as the Irvine family home. It took on the dual role as a home and state ceremonial house in 1964, when the Irvine chapter of its story closed, and the family gave it to the state for a governor's residence. The state officially accepted the gift in 1965.

Introduction

3

The foyer

It's a house where public and private lives merge...

In January 1991, Governor Arne Carlson, First Lady Susan Carlson, and their daughters Anne and Jessica, became the sixth governor's family to move into the country-manor-style house. They brought along Jenny, the family schnauzer and Bandit, their cat. A year and a half later, they adopted Jessica's pet, Daisy, a West Highland Terrier. Their son Tucker, who now makes his home in St. Paul, was living in Rhode Island at the time.

Giant step for a small girl

The move to the residence was a big change for then seven-year-old Jessica. Home for her had been a comfortable, Cape Cod style house, much like all the others in the neighborhood around Lake Owasso in Shoreview, just north of St. Paul, and not at all like the imposing structures she saw as the family drove along wide, tree-lined Summit Avenue.

"That first day here, Jessica seemed so small as she wandered through the high-ceilinged rooms on the first floor, with her hands behind her back and Jenny at her heels, exploring the place," says First Lady Susan.

"She walked from the entrance to the dining room, into the drawing room, down the few steps into the solarium, and back again into the entry way. There she stopped for the second time to look at two large, framed photos on the wall, and she asked us, 'Whose pictures are these?'

"Arne and I explained that they were photos of Mr. and Mrs. Horace Irvine, the first people to live here. She seemed

Guests fill the foyer with warmth and cheer.

Dining room

Library

...where personal mementos become pieces of history...

to accept that answer, but then glanced at them again, and with a puzzled look, said, 'Why didn't they take their pictures with them when they moved?'"

Fast paced beginning

So the Carlsons' time began in the house where public and private lives merge; where personal mementos become pieces of history; where Jessica would outgrow Cabbage Patch dolls and learn to ride her two-wheel bike; where their daughter Anne would have her wedding reception; where almost immediately their home would open to visitors from all over the state and the nation.

"We had little time to settle in," says Susan, "because we had to be ready for meetings and guests that have to do with the job of being governor — legislators and other government dignitaries."

Also, Minnesota was the sports capital of the country then. And at Governor Carlson's invitation, the premier sporting events of '91 and '92 — the Super Bowl, the World Series, the Special Olympics, the Davis Cup, and the Final Four — brought governors and their wives from North Carolina, Ohio, Georgia, Missouri, and Indiana for overnight stays.

In May of '91, Hillary Rodham Clinton, visiting the Twin Cities for a series of speeches, shared leftover chicken with the Carlsons in the kitchen and spent the night in a guest room. Later she sent a note to tell them that her stay was one of the best times she'd had, "just visiting together and sharing food . . . ." Arnold Schwarzenegger, Jessica's favorite guest, came for lunch while he was in Minnesota promoting the President's Council on Physical Fitness.

A dessert buffet in the dining room draws the attention of Jessica and the first lady.

Drawing room

Solarium

... where ordinary occurrences become special events

In addition, many children have been guests of the Carlsons. Some have come as part of a "read more" challenge the governor and first lady give students when they travel to schools around the state. Those who do additional reading get an invitation to lunch at the Governor's Residence.

"When children come, whether for occasions such as the Schwarzenegger visit, or for Easter egg hunts, Halloween and birthday parties, they always want their usual kind of food," says Susan.

But it seems special to them at the residence, she says, because the house lends a touch of elegance to even chocolate chip cookies, pizza, and hamburgers.

That elegance of yesteryear lingers, too, in the special recipes the residence chefs serve when guests come to dine. The chefs share those selected recipes on pages that follow as First Lady Susan and Governor Carlson invite you in for a glimpse of life at the residence in the '90s. With photos, bits of history, and recipes from decades past, they welcome you to stay for a look back at the times and tastes of the other families who have lived in the grand old house and made it a home to remember. ◆

Pine boughs and trees, weighted with Minnesota's snow, twinkle with fairy lights at Christmas.

The Carlson family (front row, l. to r.) Anne Carlson Davis, Jessica, First Lady Susan. Back row: Andrew Davis, Tucker Carlson, Governor Arne Carlson. Pets (l. to r.) Daisy and Jenny.

An at-home chat
with the
first lady

"We enjoy living in the residence and feel privileged to be here."

Susan Carlson

The breakfast nook in the kitchen is a favorite spot of Governor Arne Carlson and First Lady Susan. They enjoy sitting there and visiting with staff early in the morning. In fact, the governor says: "Bantering with the staff in the morning before work is probably my most favorite time of the day."

So, the nook, which nestles into one side of the kitchen, seems a fitting place to meet the first lady and talk about life at the residence, over breakfast toquitos and fresh fruit.

The room is as modern and efficient as it needs to be to provide food service for the many Governor's Residence functions. Yet, although updated and

The '90s

The governor and first lady reading with daughter Jessica in the family room

Private family room on the second floor

People appreciate having the house open again

renovated, it retains the homey feel of an early 1900s family kitchen.

The cabinet design is a copy of the original style. The counters are of Minnesota Cold Spring granite. The floor is hexagonal white ceramic tile with a gray and white checkered border, and a butler's pantry separates the kitchen from the dining room.

Susan looks very much at home in the small nook where she has a window view of the backyard lawn, flowers, and trees. She occasionally glances out to watch 10-year-old Jessica and her friend ride their bikes in the driveway as she talks about the series of open houses the Carlsons have held, and about the public tours.

The tours had not been available since 1989, and Susan says people appreciate having the house open again. "They like to hear about the Irvines and the governors and their families who've lived here — how they adapted to living in a public yet private home. I enjoy the tours, because I meet so many nice people," she says.

Living a public life

"People often ask what public life is like at the Governor's Residence. The residence is a very busy house. Last year we had more than 240 events which, in a typical week, might include three or four breakfast meetings, several lunches and at least three receptions or dinners," Susan says.

Children on a public tour of the residence receive greetings from the governor and first lady.

13

Jessica's bedroom with trolls and cello

*Susan Carlson's
third floor office*

The Carlsons want the house to reflect Minnesota culture

"It never seems to slow down here. Arne really likes to use the residence as an extension of his office. Staff, cabinet, and budget meetings are regular occurrences here. It's also a place where he can bring people together to discuss and solve problems. He used the residence extensively during the Northwest Airlines negotiations.

"But it is also a place where the state can thank and honor Minnesotans who have excelled or who have given of their time and energies in making the state a better place to live. Those kinds of receptions can vary considerably. We have honored retiring business and community leaders, volunteers for statewide charitable organizations, student essay winners, and those from the arts and athletic communities. One of my personal highlights was when we celebrated the accomplishments of S.T.R.I.D.E. recipients. These are single parents on AFDC who have successfully made strides toward economic independence and individual development.

"The state is fortunate to have such a place where Minnesotans can feel special."

Blending the now and then

The Carlsons try to blend the old-world, family-home charm of 1006 Summit with its recent history as an official governor's residence. Toward that goal, they returned the portraits of Minnesota first ladies to the wall in the downstairs conference room and added photo collages of first families from the Rolvaags to the Carlsons. In addition, the Carlsons added an elevator to give handicapped accessibility to the lower level rooms and lavatories.

The Carlsons also want the house to reflect Minnesota culture, so they've displayed selected works by Minnesota artists for public viewing. They added Native American artifacts in the house such as the dream catcher in the entry way.

"I think early Minnesota history fits with what people expect to find in a governor's house. We contacted the Historical Society to get the portrait of Henry Hastings Sibley, which once had a prominent place in the drawing room over the fireplace. We felt that the first governor's portrait is a good choice for a governor's house, and we wanted a historical portrait for the dining room, which is such a focal point in the house.

"We put together the Henry Sibley guest room on the second floor, using art and historic pieces from the Sibley era. In the lower level foyer, we assembled and hung photographs of the residence as it appeared in 1915. "We added the children's garden. I had heard about the garden

Susan Carlson visits with school children.

The first lady delights in contacts she makes with children

at the White House and thought it would be a beautiful way to honor Minnesota children, especially those who have been a part of the history of the Governor's Residence. Their names are on plaques in the garden, and as other children come to live here, their names will be there, too. The garden's dedication this year was a thrill for me."

First lady's routine

The first lady can count on a full calendar and rigorous schedule of meetings, appearances, speeches, and entertaining. Susan, a children's advocate and an attorney, has put her career on hold while she takes on the responsibilities of the first lady and manages her busy family. She has a third floor office at the residence which includes a computer that helps her organize the myriad official and family tasks she faces.

The governor calls her "Food Cop" because she uses a software package to get the nutritional breakdown on recipes and food categories to guide the family diet. "I'm running the recipes in the cookbook through the computer program, just to get the information into the book for the people who may want it. It helps in balancing nutritional and calorie intake," Susan says.

Official projects are many. Susan is honorary chair of and works closely with the 1006 Summit Avenue Society, a non-profit private citizen organization that raises funds to help preserve and refurbish the residence. She's also a member of the Governor's Residence Council and its Interior Design Committee.

Because Minnesota's children are a priority with her and the governor, Susan co-chairs the Action for Children Commission that reviews and assesses the needs and services for children in the state. A major focus of the commission is a public awareness campaign designed to foster community involvement with children's issues. She's honorary chair of the Girls' and Women's Sports Initiative, serves on the Leadership Committee of the National Governors' Spouses organization, and is a speaker on children's issues at national meetings.

Susan is on the board of the Minnesota Early Learning Development Association, the National Parenting Association Board, and serves as honorary chair of the Home Instruction Program for Preschool Youngsters. She delights in her contacts with Minnesota children and often visits libraries and schools, reading to the children.

Despite their heavy agendas, family is all-important to the Carlsons. They both go to school conferences for

Governor Carlson and Jessica enjoy time spent near brisk, blue northern waters.

Family times are cherished times

Jessica, and both help her with homework. Susan, an only daughter, is close to her mother, who has battled multiple sclerosis for several years. Although her mother lives independently, Susan schedules time for "my mom's stuff," which means anything from helping with personal records to shopping or just visiting.

Private times in public life

How do they relax, just let go when the tensions build? Susan says, " I think to really relax you have to occasionally get away. Governors' families in the past have managed to do that, because of the renovation projects, or just because of the public nature of the building. The Quies had their farm and the LeVanders had their South St. Paul home. We have a cabin.

"Here at the house, we read and listen to music in the library, pretty much as the Irvines did in the early years. We visit with our daughter Anne and our son Tucker. We may watch a movie with Jessica, or take the dogs for a walk and stop for frozen yogurt. I really like that about living here — the places we can walk to along Summit and Grand Avenues (one block south of Summit where entrepreneurs have developed a lively renaissance street).

It also helps to keep up with enjoyable hobbies, says Susan. "We brought our piano to the residence, and playing it helps Arne. He sometimes plays before breakfast and the staff says they like hearing his music early in the morning. Jessica plays the piano, too. She likes her lessons, and we try not to let anything preempt them on our schedule.

"Exercise works for me. I like to work out, walk and bike. Twice, I've gone on The Ride Across Minnesota (TRAM) which is an event to raise money for research on multiple sclerosis. This year Jessica came along, so we got to do that together.

"We enjoy living in the residence and feel privileged to be here. But, once in awhile, something happens that makes me realize it's not quite home, like the night before Easter in '93 when I awoke about 2 a.m. and remembered I hadn't hidden the Easter baskets.

"I got up, picked up the baskets, and in my pajamas, tiptoed downstairs. It was dark, and I was feeling my way on every step. I got to the bottom of the stairs and looked up into the glare of a flashlight on high beam. Our security person had appeared out of nowhere, and he really scared me. But I think I scared him just as much."

"He wasn't expecting the Easter Bunny." ◆

The Chefs

More than twenty-five years of combined schooling, training and professional experience helped to prepare Nathan Cardarelle and Kenneth Grogg for the challenges they would encounter as chefs for the Minnesota Governor's Residence. Because they are preparing gourmet-type meals for visiting dignitaries as well as cooking hot dogs and macaroni and cheese for governors' children, chefs for the residence must be flexible.

To date, the chefs say creating the recipes for *Minnesota Times and Tastes* in such a way that every cook can understand and be willing to try them, has been their biggest culinary challenge. According to Kenneth and Nathan, the joy in being a chef is the freedom of creativity. They say that perhaps the reason that these recipes had not been written down before was to insure that they would always be in a state of refinement, allowing the chef to experiment with subtle changes in flavors and textures.

The chefs encourage all cooks to enjoy these recipes, feel free to experiment and empower themselves with creative license to suit their personal tastes. ◆

Nathan Cardarelle and Kenneth Grogg pause from their work at the residence.

Take stock in the sauce

To the French-trained chefs at the residence, the sauce makes the dish. Early French culinary training involves little else but perfecting sauces. But, to make great sauce, you must first start with great stock.

Venison Stock

2¹/₂   pounds venison bones
1¹/₄   cups onion, coarsely chopped
1¹/₄   cups celery, coarsely chopped
¹/₂   cup carrots, coarsely chopped
1   head garlic, halved
6   ounces tomato paste
3   quarts water
3   cups red wine
1   bay leaf
3   sprigs fresh thyme

Preheat oven to 450 degrees. Place bones in roasting pan: roast in oven until very dark but not black. Drain excess fat from pan. Add chopped vegetables, garlic and tomato paste; roast 30 minutes. Deglaze roasting pan with red wine; add to stockpot with bay leaf and thyme. Starting with cold water, bring to boil, skimming grease frequently. Reduce heat and simmer slowly for 8 hours; strain.

Brown Veal Stock

5   pounds veal bones
2   cups chopped onions
2   cups chopped celery
1   cup chopped unpeeled carrots
1   head garlic, halved
1   can (6-ounce) tomato paste
1   tablespoon black peppercorns
6   sprigs fresh parsley
1   bay leaf
1   cup white wine
1¹/₂   gallons cold water

Heat oven to 350 degrees. Place veal bones in roasting pan. Brown bones in oven until very dark but not black. Drain fat from roasting pan; add vegetables and garlic. Return to oven for about 25 minutes. Remove bones and vegetables from roasting pan; place in stockpot and stir in tomato paste. Add peppercorns, parsley and bay leaf. Deglaze roasting pan with wine; add mixture to stockpot. Add cold water and bring to gentle boil. Cook for at least 6 to 8 hours.

A "white" stock refers to any stock that is made by the slow cooking of bones: chicken, veal, beef or fish, and vegetables. A "brown" stock refers to stocks that contain bones that have been first roasted dark brown with vegetables and tomato paste: veal, beef, venison or pheasant. Always start stock with cold water, as this will draw juices from both bones and vegetables.

*Guests enjoying their
lunch at the Spring
Fashion Show*

Menu

1006 Summit Avenue Society
Fashion Show and Luncheon
May 21, 1993

Cold Poached Salmon with Aurore Sauce*

Pineapple and Turkey Salad*

Tortellini Antipasto Salad

Sliced Tomato with Gorgonzola

Shrimp and Crab Cocktail

Fruit Tray

Assorted Bread

Flourless Chocolate Torte with Crème Anglaise and Raspberry Coulis**

*Recipe follows
** See index for recipe

Pineapple and Turkey Salad

5	cups cooked turkey, chopped
2	cups celery, chopped
1/2	cup sliced almonds, toasted
2	cups fresh pineapple, chopped
1/2	teaspoon onion powder
	salt and pepper
1-2	cups mayonnaise (add 1 cup then add only enough more to reach desired consistency)

Combine ingredients; season to taste. Serve on bed of lettuce or in pineapple shell.

8 servings as main course.

Use only homemade or commercial mayonnaise. Salad dressing overpowers the turkey.

Aurore Sauce

1/3	cup mayonnaise
1/4	cup ketchup
2	tablespoons half-and-half
6	drops Tabasco sauce

Blend all ingredients; chill. Serve with salmon, lobster or shrimp.

Can be made earlier in the day.

Susan, Anne, and Jessica enjoy afternoon festivities in period costumes at the 80th anniversary of the house.

Menu

Summer Fare
A Celebration of the 80th Anniversary of the Governor's Residence
July 24, 1991

Galantine of Duck   Roasted Red Bell Pepper and Spinach Timbale

Walleye and Salmon Mousse with Sauce Verte

Duboeuf Saint Veran, 1990

Beef Tenderloin Medallions with Wild Minnesota Mushrooms and Sauce Bordelaise

Petite Summer Vegetables

Linguine Michelina

Aegociants Pinot Noir, 1989

Salad of Mixed Greens with Raspberry Walnut Vinaigrette

Fresh Bread and Montrachet

Saint Michael, Brut Non Vintage

Flourless Chocolate Torte with Crème Anglaise and Raspberry Coulis*

Cordials

* Recipe follows

Flourless Chocolate Torte

1   **cup unsalted butter, plus a little extra for preparing pan**
6   **ounces semi-sweet chocolate squares**
3   **ounces unsweetened chocolate squares**
1¼ **cups sugar, plus a little extra for preparing pan**
5   **eggs, beaten**
    Créme Anglaise
    Raspberry Coulis

Using unsalted butter, grease 9-inch springform pan and lightly dust with sugar. Wrap foil around base of pan. Preheat oven to 375 degrees. Melt butter and chocolates in double boiler, stirring constantly until smooth. Stir together sugar and eggs until well blended; add chocolate mixture and stir until blended. Pour into prepared pan; set into larger pan into which ½-inch of water has been poured. Bake about 1 hour or until top is firm and knife inserted in center comes out clean. Refrigerate. Serve chilled or at room temperature with *Crème Anglaise and Raspberry Coulis.*

1 torte.

Use the best baking chocolate available.

Crème Anglaise

12 **egg yolks**
1½ **cups sugar**
1   **vanilla bean**
1   **quart milk**

In large mixing bowl, cream together egg yolks, sugar, and vanilla bean pulp (cut bean lengthwise, then scrape out pulp; save pod). In a large saucepan, bring milk and bean pod to boil; gradually pour half into egg mixture and stir. Return egg yolk and milk mixture to saucepan. Stirring constantly, cook over low heat until sauce coats the back of the spoon (do not boil). Chill.

Makes approximately 4 cups.

Serve with Poached Pears, Grand Marnier Soufflé or Flourless Chocolate Torte.

Raspberry Coulis

1   **cup prepared simple syrup**
3   **cups raspberries**

Pureé raspberries in blender; mix with cooled syrup. Run through a fine sieve.

To prepare simple syrup, combine 1 cup water and 1 cup sugar in saucepan. Bring to a boil; cool.

Menu

Holiday
Buffet Lunch

Grilled Chicken with Honey Thyme Sauce

Chestnut Stuffing*

Rice Pilaf

Baked Acorn Squash

Fruit Tray

Salad Lorette

Camembert with Lingonberries

French Bread

Assorted Tartlettes

Hot Apple Cider

* Recipe follows

Chestnut Stuffing

12-16 **ounces sage breakfast**
 sausage

$^1/_2$ **cup diced leeks**

$^1/_2$ **cup diced carrots**

$^1/_2$ **cup sliced green onions**

$^1/_2$ **cup diced celery**

$^1/_2$ **cup sliced mushrooms**

8 **ounces chestnuts**
 (can or jar)

 salt and pepper

$^1/_4$ **teaspoon garlic powder**

4 **cups chicken stock or**
 canned broth

1 **tablespoon chopped fresh**
 parsley

8 **cups bread cubes**

Brown sausage in large skillet or Dutch oven. Drain off three-quarters of grease. Add vegetables; sauté until onions are limp, but not brown. Add chestnuts. Season with salt, pepper and garlic powder. Stir in chicken stock. Heat to boiling. Remove from heat; stir in parsley and bread cubes; cover. Let stand for 5 minutes.

10 servings.

If stuffing is too moist, add more bread cubes or bake in oven for 15 minutes uncovered.

Menu

Community Leaders
Plated Dinner

October 19, 1993

Cheese Puffs

Herring & Crackers

Stuffed Mushrooms

Fettucini Carbonara*

Veal Piccata*

Braised Vegetables**

Boiled New Potatoes

Crepes Suzette

*Recipe follows
**See index for recipe

Frettucini Carbonara

18	ounces fresh fettucini, uncooked
4	slices pancetta
1	teaspoon minced garlic or 1 clove, crushed
1	cup dry white wine
1	pint cream
1	egg yolk, beaten
1	cup freshly grated Parmesan cheese
	salt

Cook fettucini as directed on the package. Drain, reserving 1 cup cooking water. Keep warm while preparing sauce. Slice pancetta into small pieces and cook slowly in sauté pan over medium heat. Drain grease; add garlic and quickly sauté but do not brown. Deglaze pan with white wine and reduce mixture by half. Add cream; continue cooking until sauce begins to thicken. Add fettucini to sauce along with 1 cup of pasta cooking water. Add egg yolk. Stir until mixture thickens; remove from heat. Add Parmesan while stirring constantly. Add salt to taste.

8 servings.

Pancetta is Italian bacon, available at Italian markets and some grocers. Fresh pasta cooks in only a few minutes; dried pasta takes 10 to 15 minutes.

Veal Piccata

¹/₂-1	cup all-purpose flour
	salt and pepper
2	pounds veal cutlets (4-6 ounces each)
2	large eggs, beaten
1-2	cups bread crumbs
2	large lemons (or 3 to 4 small lemons)
¹/₄	cup drained capers
¹/₂	cup fresh parsley, minced
12	tablespoons unsalted butter
4	tablespoons olive oil

Dredge veal in mixture of flour, salt and pepper; dip veal into eggs, then into bread crumbs. Peel lemon, remove seeds and membranes; dice lemon. Heat 6 tablespoons of butter and the olive oil in large skillet; brown veal on both sides. Remove veal from skillet and keep warm. Add remaining 6 tablespoons butter to skillet and heat until golden. Add parsley, lemon and capers; stir just enough to blend ingredients. Pour sauce over veal and serve immediately.

8 servings.

If your skillet can't hold all the veal at once, use half of the mixture of melted butter and oil and sauté in two batches.

Menu

Wild Game Buffet Dinner

March 9, 1992

Cold Poached Salmon

Creamed Herb Pheasant*

Duck Salmi

Stuffed Venison Leg with Wild Rice

Venison Forestière*

Venison Pâté   Moose Sarma

Pommes Dauphinoise**

Jardinière Vegetables

Wild Rice Salad**

Fruit Tray

Crème Caramel

* Recipe follows

** See index for recipe

Creamed Herb Pheasant

4   **pheasants (2 pounds each)**
1¹/₂   **cups onion, chopped**
³/₄   **cup celery, chopped**
³/₄   **cup carrot, chopped**
     water to cover
2   **bay leaves**
1   **head garlic, halved**
2   **teaspoons black peppercorns**
     roux
¹/₂   **cup cream**
2   **sprigs fresh dill weed**
1   **sprig fresh tarragon**
     salt and pepper

Clean pheasants. Tie birds and place in stockpot; add chopped vegetables. Cover with water; add bay leaves, garlic and peppercorns. Bring to boil; boil slowly for 1 hour. Remove birds and cool. Strain stock through fine sieve. Prepare roux by melting 4 tablespoons butter in medium saucepan; add 4 tablespoons flour and stir until completely blended. Add 4 cups of stock to roux; stir until mixture begins to boil. Reduce heat; add cream and herbs. Return to boil; season to taste with salt and pepper. Remove meat from bones and arrange on platter. Coat with sauce.

8 servings.

Venison Forestière

3   **pounds venison tenderloin**
     salt and pepper
2   **tablespoons olive oil**
2   **tablespoons butter**
3   **springs fresh thyme**
2   **shallots, finely diced**
2   **cloves garlic, crushed**
1¹/₂   **pints mushrooms, sliced**
¹/₄   **cup brandy**
¹/₄   **cup red wine**
3   **cups venison stock****

Lightly season venison with salt and pepper. Heat oil in a preheated pan. Sear venison on all sides; remove from pan and cover. In pan drippings, melt butter. Sauté thyme, shallots, garlic and mushrooms at medium-high heat; remove from pan. Deglaze pan with brandy; flame. Add wine and bring to boil; reduce by ³/₄. In large saucepan, bring venison stock to boil; add brandy/wine sauce. Reduce to desired consistency. Return mushrooms to sauce. Season with salt and pepper to taste. Preheat oven to 350 degrees. Place venison on baking sheet and roast in oven for 10 minutes. Slice and coat with sauce.

**See index for recipe

8 servings.

1¹/₂ pints mushrooms equals approximately 3 cups.

Menu

Buffet Lunch
for the Super Bowl

January 26, 1992

Beef Tenderloin

Seafood Fried Rice

Chicken Chasseur*

Pommes Dauphinoise*

Vegetables and Dip

Fruit Tray

French Bread and Blue Cheese Mousse

Caesar Salad

Peach Bandes

* Recipe follows

Pommes Dauphinoise

3	pounds potatoes
1	pint cream
1	teaspoon minced garlic
1	teaspoon salt
$1/2$	teaspoon pepper
$1^1/2$	cups grated Swiss cheese

Preheat oven to 400 degrees. Peel and wash potatoes. Cut each in half lengthwise, then again into $1/4$-inch slices. Arrange in 8 x 13-inch baking pan; cover with cream. Stir in garlic, salt and pepper. Cover with aluminum foil. Bake 1 hour; uncover. Top with Swiss cheese; continue baking until cheese browns.

8 servings.

Chicken Chasseur

8	chicken breast halves, boneless and skinless
	flour, as needed for dusting
	salt and pepper
6	tablespoons butter
3	cups sliced fresh mushrooms
$1/4$	cup minced shallots
3-4	tablespoons brandy
$1/2$	cup white wine
2	cups veal stock**
1	tablespoon minced fresh tarragon
4	tablespoons roux**

Preheat oven to 400 degrees. Dust chicken breasts with flour and season with salt and pepper. Melt 4 tablespoons butter in preheated skillet. Brown chicken in butter. (If you have a skillet that is oven-proof, you can prepare this dish all in one pan, as the chefs have.) Drain excess butter; bake until chicken is completely cooked, about 5 to 10 minutes. Remove chicken from pan; keep warm. Add remaining 2 tablespoons of butter, mushrooms and shallots to skillet; sauté until limp. Add brandy and flame. Deglaze^ mixture and pan with white wine. Reduce in half. Add veal stock and tarragon; simmer for 5 minutes. Place a strainer on top of the sauce and thicken with 4 tablespoons roux.^ Simmer 10 minutes. Pour sauce over warm chicken and serve.

8 servings.

You can use a variety of mushrooms such as morels, chanterelles, shitake, crimini, oyster and button, as available.

**See index for recipe
^See tips on page 189

*Arnold Schwarzenegger with
the governor and first lady,
and their daughters Jessica
and Anne*

Menu

Lunch with
Arnold Schwarzenegger

October 9, 1991

Fettucini Carbonara**

Roasted Range Hens

Pommes Croquettes**

Braised Vegetables*

Poached Pears in Port Wine Sauce* with Crème Anglaise**

* Recipe follows
** See index for recipe

Braised Vegetables

3 white leeks
3 carrots, peeled
1 pound Brussels sprouts
8 heads Belgian endive
6 slices bacon
$1/2$ teaspoon salt, or to taste
1 teaspoon pepper, or to taste
$2/3$ cup white wine
2 cups chicken stock

Preheat oven to 425 degrees. Wash leeks thoroughly; cut in half, then cut into 2-inch segments. Slice carrots into $1/4$-inch rounds. Cut ends off Brussels sprouts. Slice endives in half and remove core. Lay bacon flat in Dutch oven or heavy skillet that can be used both on the stovetop and in the oven. Layer leeks across bacon; top with carrots and Brussels sprouts. Cover with endive halves. Season with salt and pepper. Pour white wine and chicken stock over all ingredients. Cover; heat to boiling on stovetop. Bake for 30 to 45 minutes or until vegetables are tender.

10 servings.

To cut the bitterness of the endive, sprinkle sparingly with sugar before cooking.

Poached Pears in Port Wine Sauce
with Crème Anglaise

8 Bosc pears
3 cups port wine
1 cup sugar
   Crème Anglaise**

Peel pears from bottom to top. Cut small slice from bottom of each to let pears stand upright. Place pears in large saucepan. Combine port wine and sugar; pour over pears. Bring to a boil; reduce heat and simmer uncovered for 1 hour and 15 minutes. Using slotted spoon, remove pears from cooking sauce to cooling rack. Continue to reduce sauce until very thick, about $1/2$ cup. Serve pears with port wine sauce; drizzle with *Crème Anglaise.*

**See index for recipe

8 servings.

Choose a saucepan that allows the pears to stand upright, but one that is not too wide or too deep. The wine mixture should just cover pears; add water if necessary but do not dilute too much.

Cooking tips

◆ Always preheat a pan first, then add oil or butter and add food when the oil is hot. Foods won't stick or absorb too much oil.

◆ Use cookware that can go from stovetop to oven or broiler.

◆ In the recipes the chefs provided ('90s section), milk is whole milk; cream is heavy whipping cream; and butter is unsalted butter.

◆ When veal stock is not available, substitute canned beef consommé. When chicken stock is not available, substitute canned chicken broth.

◆ Toast sesame, cumin, fennel, celery seeds or rosemary in a dry pan over low heat; when toasted, add a touch of butter or oil and toss with vegetables.

◆ After juicing a lemon or orange, place the fruit pieces in a plastic bag and store in the freezer to grate later when a recipe calls for it.

◆ When separating eggs, if a little egg yolk drops into the white, moisten a cloth with cold water and dab the yolk.

◆ Place sliced apples, pears or peaches in 7-Up to prevent them from turning brown until you're ready to use them in a recipe.

◆ When cooking Belgian endive, or other bitter tasting vegetables, a pinch of sugar during the cooking process will help cut the bitterness. ◆

French Onion Soup

4	cups onion (approximately 3 large)
½	cup plus 2 tablespoons butter
2	quarts water
	salt and pepper
8	slices French bread, dry or toasted
3	cups shredded lowfat Swiss cheese

Cut onions into rings, slice or dice. Melt butter in sauté pan. Add onions to pan and brown very slowly until onions are "caramelized."^ Deglaze pan with a little water. Pour onions into saucepan, add pan drippings and remaining water; bring to boil, reduce heat and simmer for 30 minutes. Season to taste with salt and pepper. Ladle into bowls. Top with 1 slice French bread and Swiss cheese. Brown cheese under broiler.

8 servings.

^See tips on page 189

Cajun Blue Cheese Potatoes

3	pounds potatoes
¼	cup oil
2	tablespoons unsalted butter
1	tablespoon Cajun spice
4	ounces blue cheese, crumbled
	salt and pepper

Peel and wash potatoes. Cut into small pieces. Heat oil in preheated large skillet or Dutch oven. Sauté potatoes until they begin to brown. Remove excess oil; add butter and Cajun spice. Toss carefully in skillet until spice evenly coats potatoes. Cook over medium-high heat until potatoes are tender but not mushy. Add blue cheese; melt and stir. Season with salt and pepper to taste.

8 servings.

Cajun spice is available in most local grocery stores. Residence chefs use Chef Paul Prudhommes' Cajun Blackened Redfish Magic.

Pommes Croquettes

Make sure oil is very hot to keep potatoes from sticking.

2¹/₂ pounds potatoes
5 tablespoons butter
4 egg yolks
   salt and pepper
4· whole eggs
¹/₄ cup milk
³/₄ cup flour
5 cups bread crumbs
   vegetable oil, as needed

Peel, wash and quarter potatoes. Starting with cold water, set potatoes to boil in large pot with enough water to cover. When cooked, pass potatoes through a sieve or food mill. Place potatoes in large bowl. Blend in butter and egg yolks; season to taste with salt and pepper. Using pastry bag fitted with large round tip, pipe potatoes onto cookie sheet in long rows. Refrigerate 1 hour. Beat 4 whole eggs with ¹/₄ cup milk. Cut potato rows into 1¹/₂-inch pieces. Dip potato pieces first into flour, then egg wash, then bread crumbs. Chill until needed. Heat oil, enough to cover potatoes, to 350 degrees. Fry until potatoes are golden brown.

Nantais Butter

To prevent sauce from "breaking" or separating, keep temperature above 175 degrees, but below boiling.

2-3 shallots, chopped
4 cups dry white wine
35 whole black peppercorns
1 bay leaf
¹/₄ cup heavy cream
1 pound unsalted butter, cut into small pieces
   salt and pepper

In 2-quart saucepan, combine shallots, wine, peppercorns and bay leaf. Bring to a boil. Lower heat and simmer, reducing the sauce to approximately ¹/₂ cup. Add cream and return to boil; reduce heat and simmer. Over medium heat, gradually add small pieces of cold butter; blend well. Strain sauce through fine sieve. Add salt and pepper to taste.

Vegetable Strata

1	cup broccoli flowerets
1	cup cauliflower flowerets
3	tablespoons olive oil
1/2	cup carrots, julienne sliced
1/2	cup sliced green onions
1/2	cup diced red bell peppers
1	teaspoon minced garlic, or 1 clove, crushed
1	cup fresh mushrooms, sliced
1	loaf (1-pound) white bread, cut into 1 x 1-inch cubes
1/2	cup Parmesan cheese, grated
1	cup shredded Cheddar cheese
10	eggs, beaten
2 1/2	cups whole milk
1/2	teaspoon salt, or to taste
1/4	teaspoon white pepper, or to taste
1/4-1/2	teaspoon ground red (cayenne) pepper, or to taste

Blanch broccoli and cauliflower; drain and refrigerate. Heat olive oil in medium sauté pan; sauté carrots, onions, peppers and garlic until limp but not brown. Add mushrooms and sauté briefly. Grease a 13 x 9 x 2-inch baking dish. Arrange half of bread cubes in baking dish; layer with half of vegetables and half of cheeses. Repeat layers. Combine eggs, milk and seasonings; beat well. Carefully pour milk mixture into baking dish; cover with plastic wrap and refrigerate at least 8 hours; remove from refrigerator at least 1 hour before baking. Preheat oven to 375 degrees. Bake strata on center rack for about 40 minutes or until center has set.

8 to 10 servings.

To blanch vegetables, plunge them into boiling water briefly, then into cold water to stop the cooking process.

Lobster Salad with *Aurore Sauce*

4	lobsters (about 1¼ pounds each), cooked and shelled
2	heads red leaf lettuce
4	bunches Belgian endive
8	cherry tomatoes, cut in half
8	hard boiled eggs, sliced
4	avocados, sliced
	*Aurore Sauce***

Prepare Aurore Sauce. Chop lettuce; divide and place on 8 individual plates. Garnish with endive leaves, cherry tomatoes, egg and avocado slices. Split lobster tails in half, from end to end. Top each salad with one lobster claw and half of a tail. Serve with *Aurore Sauce*.

Serves 8.

Cooked Whole Lobster

4	lobsters (whole)
12	quarts water
3	carrots, coarsely chopped
5	celery stalks, coarsely chopped
2	onions, coarsely chopped
40	whole peppercorns

Clean lobsters. In a 16-quart stockpot, bring water to a boil. Add remaining ingredients; return to boil. Immerse lobsters in boiling stock; return to boil. Boil for 8 minutes. Remove lobsters from heat; cool.

**See index for recipe

Breakfast Toquitos

$^1/_2$ **pound breakfast sausage, regular or light**

8   **eggs**

8   **flour tortillas (8-inch)**

8   **ounces mild Cheddar cheese, shredded**

   picante sauce, to taste

   salt and pepper, if desired

In 10-inch skillet, brown sausage; drain if necessary. In medium bowl, beat eggs together; scramble in skillet. Combine with cooked sausage. Salt and pepper to taste. Heat tortillas over direct heat in an ungreased skillet. Place 1 ounce of cheese in center of tortilla; cover with about 2 tablespoons egg/sausage mixture and roll up burrito style. Serve with picante sauce.

8 servings.

To reduce fat content, use light sausage; brown in non-stick skillet and use very thin tortillas.

Eggs Shepard

8   **eggs**

4   **whole tomatoes**

2   **teaspoons Cajun spice**

   salt

1   **tablespoon olive oil**

8   **slices whole wheat bread**

   black pepper

Poach eggs; keep warm. Cut tomatoes into $^1/_2$-inch slices; season with Cajun spice and salt. Add olive oil to preheated saucepan; sauté tomatoes quickly, until spices are slightly brown. Toast bread. Place a slice of tomato on each piece of toast and cover with poached egg. Finish with a pinch of black pepper.

8 servings.

The chefs created this recipe for First Lady Susan Shepard Carlson. It's a favorite!

Coq au Vin

In place of chicken breasts, you can use any part of the chicken.

8	chicken breasts (4 ounces each)
1/4	pound slab bacon
2	tablespoons oil
1	tablespoon butter
20	baby onions
1/2	pound mushrooms, quartered
1/4	cup flour
4	tablespoons tomato paste
1	cup red wine
1 1/2	cups chicken stock or broth

Marinade:

2-3	cups red wine (enough to cover chicken)
1	onion, diced
1	carrot, diced
1	celery stick, diced
1/2	head garlic
1	teaspoon peppercorns
1	bay leaf
2	sprigs fresh thyme

Combine all marinade ingredients, mix well; pour over chicken breasts and refrigerate overnight or for at least 8 hours. Preheat oven to 350 degrees. Cut bacon into small cubes. Heat oil and butter in sauté pan; add bacon and fry until brown; drain and reserve for garnish. Remove chicken from marinade and pat dry. Place skin-side down in sauté pan and cook until brown. Turn and brown other side. Remove from pan. Add onions; brown and remove. Add mushrooms; sauté and remove. Discard all but 2 tablespoons of oil. Add flour and tomato paste. Deglaze^ with 1 cup red wine. Transfer chicken and sauce to saucepan or Dutch oven; add chicken stock. Bring to a boil on stove, then place in preheated oven for 40 to 60 minutes. Remove chicken to casserole or serving dish; cover and keep warm. Reduce sauce on stove until thickened and sauce coats the back of a spoon; strain. Add bacon, onions and mushrooms to casserole dish. Cover with remaining sauce and serve.

8 servings.

^See tips on page 189

Filet Gorgonzola

2 tablespoons olive oil

8 beef tenderloin filets
(6 ounces each)

1 tablespoon unsalted butter

2 shallots, finely chopped

¼ cup cognac or brandy

8 ounces Gorgonzola cheese,
crumbled

3 cups veal stock** or beef
consommé (with gelatin)

salt and pepper

Preheat large skillet; add olive oil and heat. Add filets and sauté to desired doneness. Remove filets from skillet; keep warm. Drain excess olive oil. Add butter and shallots; sauté until clear. Deglaze^ skillet with cognac or brandy. Add cheese and melt over low heat. Add stock and reduce until desired consistency. Season with salt and pepper. Return filets to sauce and turn to coat.

8 servings.

Lamb Pebronetta

2 pounds leg of lamb, trimmed

3 tablespoons olive oil

2 cups julienne strips of red
bell pepper

2 tablespoons minced shallots

1 ounce fresh basil, minced

1 tablespoon minced garlic

½ cup lamb stock or beef
consommé

salt and pepper

Cut lamb into julienne strips. Heat olive oil in large heavy sauté pan over high heat; sauté lamb quickly until no longer red. Add red pepper, shallots, basil and garlic; sauté until pepper is limp. Add stock; cook over moderate heat for 2 minutes to reduce. Season with salt and pepper.

8 servings.

Serve with roasted potatoes or couscous.

**See index for recipe
^See tips on page 189

Veal Marsala

16 veal medallions (about 3 ounces each)

salt and pepper

2 tablespoons flour, plus flour for dredging

2 tablespoons olive oil

2 tablespoons unsalted butter, divided

2 shallots, sliced

3 ounces prosciutto (Italian ham), julienne sliced

1 cup Marsala wine

3 cups *Veal Stock*** or beef consommé (with gelatin)

Lightly pound veal medallions on both sides between 2 pieces of plastic wrap. Season with salt and pepper. Dredge in flour. Heat olive oil and 1 tablespoon butter in preheated sauté pan. Brown veal on both sides; remove and set aside. Drain grease. Add 1 tablespoon of butter to pan. Sauté sliced shallots until limp, but not brown. Add prosciutto. Add 2 tablespoons flour; stir. Add Marsala and flame. When Marsala reduces by one-half, add veal stock and bring to a boil. Reduce to desired thickness. Return veal to pan and turn to coat both sides. Serve medallions coated with sauce.

8 servings.

Pepper Steak

8 beef tenderloin filets (about 6 ounces each)

cup cracked black peppercorns

salt

2 tablespoons olive oil

1 tablespoon butter

2 shallots, finely chopped

1/2 cup brandy

3 cups *Veal Stock*** or beef consommé (with gelatin)

1/2 cup cream

Press one side of each filet in cracked peppercorns; lightly dust with salt. Heat olive oil in large preheated skillet; starting with peppered side down, sauté filets to desired doneness. Remove filets from skillet; keep warm. Drain excess olive oil from skillet; add butter and shallots. Sauté shallots until limp, but not brown. Add brandy; flame. When brandy is reduced by one-half, add stock and bring to a boil. Reduce by one-third; add cream and heat to boiling. Cook and stir until mixture is reduced to coating consistency; season to taste. Return filets to skillet; coat with sauce and serve.

8 servings.

**See index for recipe

Beer Batter Pan Fish

24	ounces beer
3	cups all purpose flour
1½	teaspoons Cajun spice
1½	teaspoons salt
4	egg whites
	vegetable oil for frying
3	pounds pan fish fillets (walleye, perch, sunfish or bluefish)

Combine beer, flour, Cajun spice and salt; mix well. (It should resemble pancake batter.) Let stand for at least 30 minutes. Beat egg whites until stiff peaks form; fold into batter. Heat 2 inches of oil in a heavy sauté pan to 375 degrees. Dip fillets, one at a time, into the batter, then the oil. Cook until golden brown on both sides (it may be necessary to turn the fish if it floats).

6 to 8 servings.

Add fish in small amounts to the oil to keep a steady temperature.

Seafood Pasta Alfredo

2	quarts water
1	teaspoon salt
1	tablespoon olive oil
8	ounces penne pasta, uncooked
1	tablespoon butter
1	teaspoon minced garlic or 1 clove, crushed
2	cups chicken stock
1	cup cream, more if needed
1	egg yolk, beaten
½	pound shrimp, cooked
½	pound bay scallops, cooked
½	pound mussels, cooked
½	cup Parmesan cheese, grated
	salt and black pepper

Bring water to boil with 1 teaspoon salt and olive oil; add pasta and cook until al dente.^ Drain and keep warm. Melt butter in sauté pan. Quickly cook garlic but do not brown. Add chicken stock and reduce by one-third. Add 1 cup cream; bring to a boil. Simmer until sauce thickens (if sauce seems too thick, add a little more cream). Add egg yolk; add cooked pasta and seafood. Remove from heat. Stir in Parmesan cheese. Season with additional salt and pepper, if desired.

8 servings.

^See tips on page 189

Pork Tenderloin with *Mustard Sauce*

To prevent foods such as pork from sticking to the pan, heat the pan first, then add butter or oil. When the butter or oil is hot, add the meat. This technique also will prevent foods from absorbing too much butter or oil.

2   **pounds pork tenderloin, fully trimmed**
¹/₄   **cup flour**
     salt and pepper
1-2   **tablespoons butter**
1-2   **tablespoons vegetable oil**
     Mustard Sauce

Slice pork into 2-inch pieces; cover with plastic wrap and pound until half-inch thick. Dredge^ in flour; season with salt and pepper. Heat butter and oil in large preheated skillet. Sauté pork until golden on both sides, about 3 minutes per side. Serve with *Mustard Sauce*.

8 servings.

Mustard Sauce

4   **cups white wine**
2   **shallots, diced**
25   **peppercorns**
1   **bay leaf**
1   **cup *Veal Stock*** or consommé**
3-5   **tablespoons roux^**
¹/₄   **cup heavy cream**
3   **tablespoons Dijon mustard**

Combine wine, shallots, peppercorns and bay leaf in medium saucepan; heat until reduced by ²/₃. Add stock and cook until reduced by ¹/₃. Stir in roux, a little at a time, until the sauce coats the back of a spoon. Stir in cream; simmer for 5 minutes. Turn off heat; thoroughly stir in mustard. Strain sauce, removing peppercorns and bay leaf. Serve warm.

** See index for recipe
^See tips on page 189

Scallop Ragoût *with Saffron Rice*

2	**pounds sea scallops**
1	**zucchini**
1	**yellow squash**
2	**carrots, peeled**
1	**leek**
1	**shallot, minced**
2	**cloves garlic, minced**
2	**tablespoons butter**
1½	**cups** *Nantais Butter***
	salt and white pepper
	Saffron Rice

Rinse and clean scallops; soak in ice water for 1 hour. Using melon baller, make vegetable balls from zucchini and yellow squash; slice or julienne carrots and whites of the leek. Remove scallops from water; pat dry. Slice into medallions. In a large skillet, sauté scallops in butter over low heat until they begin to "sweat." Add vegetables, garlic and shallots, cooking until they are crisp-tender. Blend in *Nantais Butter*. Salt and pepper to taste. Serve with *Saffron Rice*.

8 servings.

To "sweat" means after the scallops have sautéed for a few minutes, they will begin to produce beads of water.

Saffron Rice

4	**cups white stock or chicken broth**
1	**bay leaf**
1	**teaspoon salt, optional**
¼	**gram saffron**
2	**cups short- or long-grain rice, uncooked**
3-4	**tablespoons butter**
1	**teaspoon pepper, or to taste**

Combine stock, bay leaf and salt in a large saucepan; heat to boiling. Stir in saffron and rice; return to boiling. Reduce heat; cover and simmer for 20 minutes. Remove from heat and add butter; do not stir. Cover and let stand for 5 minutes. Remove bay leaf. Stir in salt and pepper to taste.

**See index for recipe

Pecan Lace Cups *with Glazed Berries*

Coarsely chopped pecans allow the dough to form "lace" holes, letting the sauce pool around the cup on the plate. Do not chop them too fine. Leave plenty of room between cookies because they spread. It may be necessary to bake in 2 batches.

1	cup brown sugar, packed
1/2	cup light corn syrup
12	tablespoons unsalted butter
1	teaspoon salt
1	cup flour
1	cup pecans, coarsely chopped
	ice cream
	Glazed Berries

Preheat oven to 425 degrees. Melt brown sugar, corn syrup, butter and salt in medium saucepan. Remove from heat. Add flour and pecans. Place 1 tablespoon of mixture on cookie sheet well greased with unsalted butter. Bake until golden brown, about 10 to 12 minutes. When mixture begins to cool, remove each cookie from cookie sheet with metal spatula and place each over an upside-down glass custard cup (³/4 cup size). When cool and solid, remove lace cups. Refrigerate until serving. Fill with ice cream and *Glazed Berries*.

8 servings.

Glazed Berries

Fresh berries are preferred, but you can use frozen.

2	cups sugar
1¹/2	cups water
1/2	pint strawberries, halved
1	pint blueberries
1	pint raspberries or blackberries

In a large sauté pan or skillet, heat sugar and water over medium heat until thick, shiny and barely boiling. Add strawberries and blueberries. Cook slowly until berries soften slightly and syrup becomes colored by juice. Add raspberries; toss quickly. Cool. Spoon generously over vanilla ice cream in *Pecan Lace Cups*. Sauce will pool around Pecan Lace Cup.

Grand Marnier Soufflé

2   cups *Pastry Cream*
3   tablespoons cocoa
3   tablespoons Grand Marnier
8   egg whites
1/2 teaspoon cream of tartar

Preheat oven to 425 degrees. Grease 8 individual soufflé dishes with unsalted butter and lightly dust with sugar. Prepare *Pastry Cream*. Add cocoa and Grand Marnier to Pastry Cream. Whip egg whites with cream of tartar until stiff. Gently fold egg whites into *Pastry Cream*. Place equal amounts of mixture into each soufflé dish and level off with spatula or knife edge. Bake for 20 to 25 minutes.

8 servings.

Serve with Crème Anglaise.

Pastry Cream

6   egg yolks
1   cup sugar
1   quart milk
8   tablespoons cornstarch

Place egg yolks in mixing bowl. With wire whisk, whip sugar into egg yolks. Continue whipping until mixture is pale in color. Boil milk in saucepan. Mix cornstarch into egg and sugar mixture. When milk boils, pour half into egg and sugar mixture; stir until well blended. Add remaining egg and sugar mixture to saucepan; return to a boil. Mixture will be very thick. Strain through a fine sieve and cover immediately with plastic wrap. Refrigerate.

4 cups.

Arne's Hot Chili

The Carlsons often prepare this family favorite at their lake cabin.

2   pounds ground beef
1   medium onion, chopped
2   teaspoons fresh minced garlic
1   cup chopped celery
2   cans (15-ounce) spicy chili beans
2   cans (15-ounce) dark red kidney beans
1   can (28-ounce) whole tomatoes
2   cans (28-ounce) tomato sauce
1   teaspoon Tabasco
2   tablespoons Worcestershire
3   tablespoons chili powder
1   teaspoon dry mustard
$1/2$ teaspoon red pepper
1   teaspoon black pepper

Brown beef in large pot and drain fat. Add onion, garlic and celery, sauté until onion is limp, but not brown. Add beans, tomatoes, and tomato sauce; mix together. Add remaining ingredients; mix thoroughly. Let simmer for 1 hour.

12 servings.

Ham Glaze a la Carlson

1   cup packed brown sugar
3   tablespoons dry sherry
2   tablespoons butter, softened
2   tablespoons flour
$1/2$ teaspoon dry mustard
$1/8$ teaspoon ground cinnamon

In small bowl, combine all ingredients until thoroughly blended. Remove ham from oven 30 minutes before it is done. Remove any skin from ham and cut fat surface lightly in uniform diamond shapes. Brush or spread with glaze. Return to oven for 30 minutes longer.

Enough glaze for a 3- to 4-pound ham.

Cipolle Spaghetti Sauce

³/₄ cup chopped onion

1 clove garlic, chopped

¹/₂ cup oil or margarine

¹/₂ cup flour

¹/₄ cup tomato paste (half of a 6-ounce can)

¹/₂ cup tomato sauce (half of an 8-ounce can)

¹/₂ teaspoon poultry seasoning

¹/₄ teaspoon nutmeg

¹/₄ teaspoon allspice

salt and pepper

3-4 cups chicken broth or bouillon

Sauté onion and garlic in oil in a large preheated skillet or Dutch oven. Lower heat to medium; add flour and cook for 5 minutes or until brown. Add tomato paste, tomato sauce, poultry seasoning, nutmeg, allspice, salt and pepper. Cook the mixture for 10 to 15 minutes; stir often to prevent sticking. Sauce will take on a shiny appearance when ready. Add chicken broth to thin sauce to desired consistency. Heat, stirring occasionally, about 30 minutes or until well blended.

4 cups.

This Northern Italian red sauce is a favorite Carlson family recipe, given to them by their lake cabin neighbor, Sue Cipolle. The recipe was handed down to Sue from her grandmother Esther Benigni. Esther Benigni (1903-1993) and her husband Joe owned and ran the Avon Inn, an Italian restaurant in Joliet, Illinois. She cooked and managed the food and he took care of the bar.

Grandma Shepard's Sour Cream Cookies

Another Carlson family favorite, this recipe is from Susan Carlson's grandmother. Frost and decorate cookies for special occasions.

2	cups sugar
1/2	cup shortening
2	eggs, beaten
1	teaspoon vanilla
5	cups flour
2	teaspoons baking powder
1	teaspoon baking soda
1	cup sour cream
	dash of salt (optional)

Preheat oven to 425 degrees. In large mixing bowl, cream sugar, shortening, eggs and vanilla until well blended. In a separate bowl, combine flour, baking powder, baking soda and salt. Add to sugar mixture, alternating with sour cream. Mix well. Divide dough into thirds. On well-floured board or pastry cloth, roll out each third into a 1/4-inch thick circle. Cut with 2-inch cookie cutter. Place cookies on greased baking sheets. Sprinkle with sugar. Bake 8 to 10 minutes, or until lightly browned.

9 to 10 dozen cookies.

Arne's Swedish Pancakes

The Carlsons prefer these pancakes with light maple syrup. For traditional Swedish pancakes, top with powdered sugar, cinnamon and fresh or frozen lingonberries.

1/2	cup flour
1/8	teaspoon salt
1/2	teaspoon baking powder
1	tablespoon sugar
2	eggs, beaten
1	cup milk
3	tablespoons unsalted butter, melted
1	teaspoon vanilla

Combine flour, salt, baking powder and sugar. Add eggs; gradually beat in milk and melted butter. Stir in vanilla. Pour 3-inch circles onto hot skillet or griddle (lightly greased or nonstick). Turn over when brown.

4 to 6 servings.

Marilyn's Hot German Potato Salad

6	medium potatoes (about 6 cups diced or sliced)
6	slices bacon
1/3	cup bacon drippings
1	cup onion, chopped
3/4	cup celery, chopped
2/3	cup water
1/2	cup cider vinegar
1	teaspoon sugar
1-2	teaspoons salt, or to taste
1/4-1/2	teaspoon pepper, or to taste
2	tablespoons mayonnaise
6	green olives, sliced

Boil whole potatoes in water until tender; keep warm. In a skillet or microwave, cook bacon until crisp; crumble and set aside. Using 1/3 bacon drippings, sauté onion and celery until onion is soft, but not brown. Add the water, vinegar, sugar, salt and pepper. Boil for 2 minutes, or until slightly reduced. Slice warm potatoes. Place in large mixing or serving bowl. Pour hot dressing over potatoes; add mayonnaise and crumbled bacon; toss lightly, coating the potatoes. Garnish with sliced olives. Serve hot.

6 to 8 servings.

Marilyn Bingham is a long-time family friend who, according to Arne, makes the best hot potato salad in the country.

Susan's Meat Loaf

1	egg
1	packet dry onion soup mix
2	tablespoons skim milk
1/4	cup barbecue sauce
1/2	cup bread crumbs
3/4	teaspoon pepper
1 1/2	pounds ground beef
1	tablespoon barbecue sauce

Preheat oven to 350 degrees. Mix together first six ingredients; add ground beef. Mix thoroughly. Press mixture into loaf pan and cover with 1 tablespoon barbecue sauce. Bake for 1 hour. Drain fat before serving.

6 servings.

Arne loves this spicy version of meat loaf.

Horace and Clotilde Irvine in 1946

A look back
at the
early years

"Some of the best times I remember
were listening to the radio
in the library."

Olivia Irvine Dodge

Horace and Clotilde Irvine had been married three years when they bought the lot for their home at 1006 Summit Avenue for $7,000 in 1910. Their daughter Olivia Irvine Dodge remembers well the good life she shared with her parents, brother Thomas, and sisters Elizabeth and Clotilde in the house their parents built.

"Some of the best times I remember were those when we'd all listen to the radio in the library, my favorite room," Olivia says. "I recall one day we children asked daddy if we could listen to Bing Crosby, and he let us, but he said, 'He'll never last six weeks.' We often chuckled about that."

Remembrance

Mrs. Horace Irvine with Elizabeth (at left), Clotilde, and Thomas

Olivia Irvine Dodge
at age two

The undeveloped avenue was a fine place for a country manor

Olivia's dad was Horace Hills Irvine, a remarkable man and son of Thomas Irvine, a pioneer in Minnesota's lumber industry. With his father, Horace established the lumber firm of Thomas Irvine and Son and held interests in other corporations such as St. Paul Fire and Marine Insurance Company. He was president of Weyerhaeuser Timber Company and one of five businessmen who founded Northwest Airlines. He married Clotilde McCullough of Clinton, Iowa on October 3, 1907.

When Horace and Clotilde announced where on Summit Avenue they would build their home, some people wondered why they would build "way out on the open prairie," because the avenue in that area was relatively undeveloped. However, architect William Channing Whitney, whom Horace hired to design the house, declared it a fine place for a country manor house and drew up the plans for the future Irvine home.

No ordinary house

This would be no ordinary house. It would cost $50,000. It would have 20 rooms, 9 fireplaces, 9 bedrooms, 8 bathrooms, and 2 sleeping porches. And, although Horace was a lumberman, the house would be of brick and stone. But beautiful woods would adorn the interior: oak in the large entry hall, African mahogany in the living room, and Circassian English walnut in the dining room.

Beaux Arts style

The design would be the architect's interpretation of an English Tudor country manor in the Beaux Arts style, incorporating the best of classical architecture. It would serve as a setting for visiting dignitaries and have a yard big enough for formal gardens, vegetable plots, and outdoor parties where guests would dance on portable platforms under the glow of Japanese lanterns.

Clotilde Irvine would choose furnishings that would not be faddish or trendy, but would complement the architecture. The family moved into their new house in 1912 with their two children, Elizabeth and Thomas. Their youngest daughters, Clotilde and Olivia, were born in the master bedroom. The children's beloved nursemaid, Octavia Rocheford, or "Tay," came to live with the family when Olivia was five and stayed with Clotilde and Olivia even after they left the Summit Avenue address. "It was Tay," Olivia says, "who shed the most tears when we left the house in 1965 for the last time."

Through the years, live-in household staff helped maintain the Irvines' busy lifestyle. At times the Irvines

Mrs. Horace Irvine in her car in 1920

The Irvines stayed through a half century of social change

employed as many as seven people, including a cook, butler, waitress, upstairs maid, laundress, nursemaid, gardener, and chauffeur.

The chauffeur and his wife lived upstairs in the carriage house. The rest of the staff lived on the third floor of the main house, and each person had his or her own bed chamber. The house had a servants' dining room and a sewing room where the staff did the mending and the kids liked to spend their time with the people who saw to their every need. Olivia remembers that the servants were like extended family and often joined the Irvines in the library for those times she cherished, listening to the "wireless."

Culinary traditions

Although the Irvines preferred quiet dinner parties, they also entertained with splendor. Guests were people whose names are part of Minnesota history: the Pillsburys, McKnights, Shepards, Kelloggs, Ordways, and from time-to-time well-known celebrities, like Eleanor Roosevelt. Olivia says the children would peek under the staircase railing on the second-floor landing to watch as guests came into the entrance hall below.

On those occasions, the food was splendid, too, with menus that included caviar and entrée specialties. The family tradition, however, was to have elegant but simple, wholesome meals. A black bean soup, roast leg o' lamb, brown potatoes with gravy, and angel food cake and ice cream for dessert made up a typical Sunday dinner menu. Christmas dinner featured roast turkey with sausages and the special touches of Oyster Bisque, homemade custard ice cream, and Brandy Snaps, a family favorite.

A half century of history

The house at 1006 Summit was home to members of the Irvine family from 1912 to 1964. Their gracious style of community-minded, influential living remained their hallmark as the world went from horses and buggies to high-powered automobiles; from open prairie country manor living to metropolitan city life; from floor-length dresses and elaborate hats to mini skirts and go-go boots; from porcelain dolls to Barbie; and from homemade ice cream to instant pudding mix.

Horace Irvine died in 1947. His wife Clotilde McCullough Irvine lived in their home until she died in 1964. It was then that Olivia Irvine Dodge and Clotilde Irvine Moles, now deceased, gave the house, in memory of their parents, to the State of Minnesota for use as the Governor's Residence. ◆

Menu

The Irvines'
Favorite Sunday Supper

Black Bean Soup*

Crackers

Roast Leg O' Lamb with Mint Sauce*

Brown Potatoes and Gravy

Iced Tea

Angel Food Cake

Ice Cream

Coffee

*Recipe follows

Black Bean Soup

2   **cups dried black beans**

       beef shank bone

       cayenne pepper

       salt

10   **teaspoons sherry**

       hard-cooked egg, finely chopped

       thin lemon slices

Wash and sort black beans. Cover with water in very large kettle; soak overnight. Add 3 more quarts water and soup bone; cover and simmer for 5 to 6 hours or until beans are very tender. Add cayenne pepper and salt to taste. Pureé mixture in blender or food processor. Ladle very hot soup into individual bowls. Stir 1 teaspoon sherry into each bowl; sprinkle with egg and garnish with lemon slices.

10 servings.

Mint Sauce

1¹/₂ **tablespoons powdered sugar**

3   **tablespoons hot water**

¹/₃   **cup finely chopped fresh mint leaves**

¹/₂   **cup cider vinegar**

At least 3 hours before serving, dissolve powdered sugar in hot water; cool. Stir in mint leaves and vinegar. Serve with lamb.

1 cup.

Menu

White Bear Yacht Club
Regatta Picnic

Jellied Madrilene
Cold Baked Ham with Mustard Sauce*
Watermelon Pickles*
Rolls
Tomato Aspic with Marinated Green Beans*
Potato Salad Mold
Fresh Fruit Compote
Brownies

*Recipe follows

Mustard Sauce

2 cups light cream
2 egg yolks
3 tablespoons dry mustard
$^1/_2$ teaspoon salt
2 tablespoons flour
$^1/_2$ cup sugar
$^3/_4$ cup vinegar

Scald 1$^1/_2$ cups of the cream in medium saucepan. In small bowl, beat egg yolks; stir in remaining $^1/_2$ cup of cream. Combine egg yolk mixture and dry ingredients; stir into scalded cream. Cook until mixture is smooth and thick, stirring constantly. Boil and stir for 1 minute. Heat vinegar and stir in. Beat well; cool and serve with baked ham.

3 $^1/_2$ cups.

Watermelon Pickles

rind of a 16-pound watermelon (about 6 pounds of rind)
3 quarts cold water
$^1/_2$ cup pickling salt
boiling water
3 cups white vinegar
6 cups sugar
1 cup water
1 tablespoon whole cloves
2-3 cinnamon sticks, broken

Trim dark green and pink parts from watermelon rind; cut into 1-inch cubes. Soak rind overnight in solution of 3 quarts water and pickling salt. If more water is necessary, use the same proportion of salt to water. Drain and rinse rind. In 6- to 8-quart kettle or Dutch oven, cover rind with boiling water; cook just until tender, about 10 minutes. Meanwhile, tie spices loosely in a cheesecloth bag; place in mixture of vinegar, sugar and 1 cup water; simmer for 10 minutes. Add drained rind; simmer until watermelon rind is clear; remove spice bag. Fill hot pint jars with rind pieces and syrup, leaving $^1/_2$-inch head space. Adjust lids. Process in boiling water bath for 5 minutes.

As viewed from the front lawn of 1006 Summit Avenue, the street shows horses and carts used to transport supplies to homes.

Grand Boulevard

Monumental boulevards like Summit Avenue were popular in cities big enough and wealthy enough to accommodate them. They served as appropriate settings for large homes, often with additional land for lawn and gardens. They also provided a practical means for exercising horses. Taking horses for a drive along the avenue was an important social occasion, and the wide center strip served as a bridle path.

The avenue developed slowly, because people found it difficult to get up the hill. The construction boom occurred between 1882 and 1886 when builders put up 46 new houses. Price of land rose from $150 per front foot to $500 per front foot.

In its history, 440 homes have had a Summit Avenue address. But the unique, four-and-a-half-mile long boulevard deteriorated during the Depression years and during World War II, when owners converted many of the large old homes into apartments for returning service personnel. When people in the 1970s became interested in preservation and began restoring homes, the avenue began its return to its former grandeur. ◆

Tomato Aspic

1	envelope unflavored gelatin
2	tablespoons cold water
2	tablespoons boiling water
1	can (10 ^{3}/$_4$-ounce) condensed tomato soup
1	package (3-ounce) lemon-flavored gelatin
2	cups hot tomato juice
^{1}/$_2$	teaspoon salt

Soften unflavored gelatin in cold water, dissolve in boiling water; add tomato soup. Dissolve lemon gelatin in hot tomato juice; stir in soup mixture and salt until well mixed. Pour into 5-cup ring mold; refrigerate until set. Unmold and fill center with well-drained *Marinated Green Beans.*

8 servings.

Marinated Green Beans

1	cup olive oil
^{1}/$_3$	cup wine vinegar
1	teaspoon salt
^{1}/$_2$	teaspoon paprika
^{1}/$_4$	teaspoon dry mustard
1	teaspoon Worcestershire sauce
1	clove garlic
3	pounds fresh green beans, cooked to crisp-tender

Combine all ingredients except beans in tightly covered container; refrigerate overnight. Remove garlic clove; shake marinade well and pour over beans. Refrigerate several hours.

8 servings.

Budding photographer's dream

*E*leanor Roosevelt's visit to her home was a highlight for Olivia, who took the first lady's picture beside a photo of the president. Olivia had a collection of Democratic memorabilia Mrs. Roosevelt wanted to see. Olivia, an amateur photographer, was thrilled to have the opportunity to photograph the first lady.

Today, Olivia Dodge Irvine lives in West St. Paul where she continues to work on numerous civic-oriented projects. She is founder of the Thomas Irvine Dodge Nature Center. The center is located on 151 acres of land in the West St. Paul area and is dedicated to teaching children to love nature and to take care of it as their own. Its primary goal is to provide opportunities for learning about, enjoying, and preserving gifts of nature. ◆

Posed beside her husband's portrait, Eleanor Roosevelt sits amidst Olivia's collectibles — and reminds Olivia to use a flashbulb — as the young photographer snaps her picture.

Granny Irvine's Fudge Bars

2   **ounces unsweetened chocolate**
$^3/_4$ **cup butter or margarine**
$^3/_4$ **cup sugar**
3   **eggs**
3   **tablespoons flour**
    dash of salt
1   **teaspoon baking powder**
1   **teaspoon vanilla**
    powdered sugar

Heat oven to 375 degrees. Melt chocolate with butter; stir in sugar. Remove from heat. In medium bowl, combine eggs, one at a time, with butter and sugar mixture, beating well after each addition. Add flour, salt, baking powder and vanilla; mix well. Pour into greased 9 x 9 x 2-inch pan. Bake for 15 to 20 minutes. Do not overbake. Cut into squares while hot. Sprinkle with powdered sugar.

16 ($2^1/_4$-inch) squares.

Apple Cake

$^1/_4$ **cup butter or margarine, melted**
$^1/_4$ **cup sugar**
$^2/_3$ **cup milk**
2   **teaspoons baking powder**
2   **cups all-purpose flour**
4   **medium apples, cored and sliced**
$^1/_4$ **cup butter or margarine, melted**
$^1/_4$ **cup sugar**
$^1/_2$ **teaspoon ground cinnamon**
$^1/_4$ **teaspoon ground nutmeg**

Heat oven to 350 degrees. Combine $^1/_4$ cup butter, $^1/_4$ cup sugar, milk, baking powder and flour. Pour into greased 9 x 5 x 3-inch loaf pan. Arrange apple slices on top of batter. Combine remaining ingredients; sprinkle over apples. Bake for 55 to 65 minutes.

Makes 1 loaf.

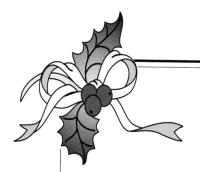

Menu

Christmas Dinner
at the Irvines

Oyster Bisque*

Celery and Crackers

Roast Turkey Surrounded with Sausages

Sweet Mashed Potatoes

Green Beans

Hot Rolls

Cranberry Jelly

Plum Pudding and Sauce

Custard Ice Cream

Brandy Snaps*

*Recipes follow

Oyster Bisque

1   **pint fresh oysters**
4   **cups light cream**
1   **slice onion**
2   **stalks celery, chopped**
1   **sprig fresh parsley**
1   **small bay leaf**
$^1/_3$ **cup butter**
$^1/_3$ **cup flour**
     salt and pepper

Drain and chop oysters. Heat oysters slowly to boiling and press through coarse sieve. Scald cream with onion, celery, parsley and bay leaf. Melt butter in saucepan; stir in flour. Strain cream (removing vegetables and herbs) into butter-flour mixture and cook over low heat, stirring until mixture bubbles and thickens. Add sieved oysters and season with salt and pepper to taste. (If a thinner soup is desired, substitute milk for light cream.)

6 servings.

To scald means to heat liquid to just below the boiling point.

Brandy Snaps

1   **cup sugar**
1   **cup butter, melted**
2   **cups molasses**
2   **cups all-purpose flour**
2   **tablespoons brandy**

Heat oven to 350 degrees. Combine all ingredients. Drop only 4 heaping teaspoonfuls of mixture onto a large ungreased cookie sheet, spacing far apart. Bake for 5 to 6 minutes. Watch carefully! Cool 3 to 5 minutes on cookie sheet; remove with wide spatula. Roll immediately around handle of a wooden spoon or shape into cones. Cool; store in airtight container.

6 dozen.

Each cookie can be filled with whipped cream or an ice cream "finger" and topped with Chocolate Sauce.

Carrot Pudding

¹/₂	cup butter or margarine, softened
¹/₂	cup sugar
1	egg
1	cup all-purpose flour
1	teaspoon baking soda
1	teaspoon ground cinnamon
1	teaspoon ground nutmeg
	dash of salt
1	cup chopped raisins
1	cup chopped walnuts
1	cup shredded carrots
1	cup shredded potatoes

Cream butter and sugar; beat in egg. Combine dry ingredients; toss with raisins and nuts. Combine all ingredients; mix well. Pour into greased 1¹/₂-quart mold; cover tightly with foil. Place mold on rack over 1 inch of boiling water in steamer or Dutch oven. Steam for 3 hours, adding more boiling water as necessary. When pudding is done, remove from steamer, uncover and unmold. Serve in wedges topped with *Butter Sauce.*

8 servings.

Butter Sauce

1	cup sugar
¹/₂	cup butter
¹/₂	cup light cream
1	teaspoon vanilla

Combine all ingredients in medium saucepan; heat to boiling over moderate heat, stirring constantly. Boil for 4 minutes; serve warm.

Cheese Rarebit

16   **ounces (4 cups) Cheddar cheese, shredded**

1   **tablespoon cornstarch**

12   **ounces beer**

1   **teaspoon prepared mustard**

1   **teaspoon Worcestershire sauce**

    toast points

    crisp bacon strips (optional)

    hard-boiled eggs, sliced (optional)

Combine cheese and cornstarch. Heat beer in fondue pot or saucepan over moderate heat. Gradually add cheese, stirring constantly until melted and mixture begins to bubble. Stir in mustard and Worcestershire sauce. Remove from heat and serve warm from fondue pot or chafing dish over toast points. If desired, garnish with strips of crisp bacon and slices of hard-cooked egg.

6 servings.

71

Governor Karl Rolvaag, First Lady Florence, and children Kristin and Paul

The decade
of
change, turmoil, war

"... One of the problems
of being governor in Minnesota
is that we've never had an official place for
dignitaries to stay."

Florence Rolvaag

Generation gap was a term of the times as young people revolted against the "establishment." Racial tension exploded into marches and rallies in cities and on campuses. An assassin's bullet took the life of President John F. Kennedy, the Vietnam War escalated, and the '60s went into history as the most violent of times for the United States since the Civil War.

The transition of the Horace Hills Irvine home to a State Ceremonial Building and the Minnesota Governor's Residence was timely and significant. Timely, because it came in an era of drastic change; significant, because it represented a lifestyle of family and tradition that people wanted to hold on to.

The '60s

Governor Rolvaag with school children in California

The house badly needed furniture suitable to its architecture

When the state officially accepted it as a gift from the Irvine family in September 1965, the legislature immediately appropriated money for restoring the house and preserving its history. In efforts to preserve the building for generations to come, repairs and reconstruction began that would go on for decades.

Rolvaag family moves in

Governor Karl F. Rolvaag, then serving his last year as governor, moved into the newly acquired residence with his wife Florence, their 16-year-old daughter Kristin, and Leo, their six-year-old beagle. Son, Paul, was a student at St. Olaf College in Northfield, which meant he escaped the first month of furious remodeling and redecorating that took place so the residence could host an October 1 visit from Crown Prince Harald of Norway.

Although Florence Rolvaag would have to endure initial renovation of the Irvine house, she saw a need for an official residence. As the legislature debated whether to accept the aging mansion, Florence told reporters: "One of the problems of being governor in Minnesota is that we've never had an official place for visiting dignitaries to stay. We've had to accommodate them . . . and do our entertaining in hotels."

Because the Irvines had taken most of their furnishings with them when they left the house, it badly needed furniture suitable to its style and architecture. John Myers, chairperson of Hoerner-Waldorf and friend of the Irvine family, offered to help; and he found furnishings to borrow.

With that problem solved, decorators and artisans hurriedly readied a guest bedroom for Prince Harald on the second floor, directly over the library.

However, when royal protocol required an adjoining room for the aide to the prince, plans changed. The Norwegian ambassador occupied the newly readied guest room. The prince used young Kristin's bedroom, and his aide slept in the room next to it.

Furniture, renovation

The visit was a success, and when the prince left, Mrs. Rolvaag returned the borrowed furnishings to their owners. Then she again called on John Myers who set up a small, unofficial nonpartisan committee. The volunteer group asked old Minnesota families to donate furniture for the house, and Myers said "within a couple of years" they had collected enough to make the residence "entertainable."

The LeVander family (l. to r.): Jean LeVander King, Tom King, Governor Harold LeVander, First Lady Iantha, Dyan, Hap, and Carla Augst LeVander

First family lives with disruption of remodeling, renovation

The appropriation from the legislature and privately donated work and materials paid for renovation and redecorating in the kitchen and basement, baths, and third-floor rooms. For a year, the Rolvaags put up with the mess and disruption that comes with a major overhaul.

Workers replastered, added new ceramic tiles and updated bath fixtures, installed new lighting, furnishings, and carpeting. The Minneapolis Art Institute, the St. Paul Art Center, and a Hastings antique dealer provided on-loan paintings, art objects, and antique furniture.

Heritage shines through

The Rolvaags brought a strong Norwegian influence to the house. Many pictures, wall hangings, and decorative pieces, including pewter bowls, were family heirlooms or purchases from a trip through Scandinavian countries.

Mrs. Rolvaag did all of the family cooking, except for large parties, and stocked the kitchen with utensils and dishes from the family's Arden Hills home. With help from a St. Paul interior designer, she made final decisions about rugs, furnishings, and other decorations suitable to the residence.

She selected Lenox china in the Tuxedo pattern for use in the dining room. The service plates have the state seal in the center, and they still grace the residence table on official and special occasions. Ironically, Mrs. Rolvaag didn't use the china she chose; the actual purchase didn't occur until the LeVander and Anderson administrations.

Renovation, entertainment mix

The family of Governor Harold LeVander and First Lady Iantha LeVander was the second governor's family to become residents of the house as renovations continued full force. Before they officially moved in, however, the first lady managed to hold an afternoon tea for the Dome Club of Minnesota during a brief respite from the hammering and sawing. The wives of more than 200 officials — Minnesota legislators, Supreme Court justices, and constitutional officers — attended.

A legislative appropriation of $230,000 kept the remodeling on schedule. Inside the house, workers updated plumbing, electrical wiring, and heating. They installed air conditioners and laid a parquet floor in the basement. Outside, they poured concrete into which Mrs. LeVander pressed several of her husband's "Heralder" campaign buttons. They added a parking lot, sidewalks, and a fence around the entire property. Some of the money helped

Governor Harold LeVander at the podium and First Lady Iantha in the front row at the dedication of
"Man Nam" Vietnam Memorial on the residence grounds

First Lady chooses state colors, blue and gold for theme of decor

pay for permanent furnishings to add to those the Irvines had left behind and to the fine pieces individuals and foundations had donated.

Working, living house

Iantha LeVander wanted the residence to incorporate Minnesota history and lore into a "simple but elegant working, living house," serving as both a governor's residence and a site for state functions, but she wanted it to "look like a governor's house."

With that in mind, she chose a decor that used the state colors, blue and gold, combined with soft shades of green. And the state Star of the North emblem appeared prominently on a beige circular rug in the solarium and on a blue and gold rug at the entry door. The Royal Danish flatware by International, Romance crystal, and Lenox china that Mrs. Rolvaag and her committee had selected completed purchases the state made for the interior of the residence.

The LeVanders worked around the remodeling, took advantage of breaks in the tumult, and entertained diplomats, royalty, and politicians with a flair. When French ambassador Charles Lucet visited, Mrs. LeVander bought French music recordings to play.

She planned a luncheon reception for England's Princess Alexandra and her husband Lord Angus Ogilvy, who were on a promotional tour for British fashions. Because of the renovation in process, the first lady was relieved to hear that protocol wouldn't allow the press in to take photos during lunch.

The reception for Norway's King Olav V in May of 1968 was at the State Capitol, because the residence was undergoing the heaviest part of the '60s renovations, which stopped long enough for Jean LeVander and Thomas King to have their wedding reception. The event was the first such celebration at the residence. The second was Harold, Jr. (Hap), and his bride, Carla Augst's reception, three years later.

War casts a shadow

The LeVanders were able to retreat to their own home in South St. Paul, away from the clutter, smells, and sounds of remodeling, and many festive official and family gatherings brightened their tenure at the residence. But, nevertheless, Mrs. LeVander refers to their time as "sad years."

"The Vietnam War was at its height while we lived at the residence. Nationally, families, colleges, institutions,

"Man Nam" sculpture honors Vietnam War servicemen and women.

A daughter leaves a horseshoe as a good luck wish

and churches were affected by it. It had a great influence on Minnesota's institutions and people."

Deeply moved by the personal sacrifices the war asked many Minnesotans to make, the first lady led a project that raised funds to commission Minnesota sculptor Paul T. Granlund to create a monument in honor of those who served in Vietnam. Donors to the project from throughout the state and the families of the servicemen and women attended the dedication of Granlund's creation, "Man Nam," on September 27, 1970. The sculpture on the front lawn is the focal point of a long-term landscaping project that puts many varieties of Minnesota wildflowers and trees on display at the residence.

Good luck wish

When the LeVanders moved out in January of 1971, daughter Dyan left a horseshoe in her bedroom to wish good luck to the new tenants. Dyan, now a minister at a Lutheran church near Madison, Wisconsin, was 13 when her family moved to 1006 Summit.

Mrs. LeVander had a housekeeper to manage their South St. Paul home, because her elderly father lived with the family. That meant that Dyan also could spend much of her time there, ride her horse, and be with friends.

She did, however, transfer from her South St. Paul public school to Minnehaha Academy. Her parents had a graduation party for her amid twinkling outside lights on the grounds at the Governor's Residence.

The next occupants, Governor Wendell and First Lady Mary Anderson converted Dyan's room into their master bedroom.

The horseshoe is still in the house. ◆

Mrs. LeVander plays with family pet, Putty.

81

The Governor's Garden

Outside the residence grow a wide variety of native Minnesota ferns including ostrich, lady, interrupted, berryladders, and maidenhair.

The residence garden shows off fringed loosestrife, the dogtooth violet, wild columbine, Solomon's seal, bloodroot, blue flag, and iris. These are all Minnesota wildflowers contributed by nurseries in Askov and Grand Rapids.

Colorado spruce, flowering crab, barberry, dogwood, hemlock, tallhedge, buckthorn, locust, spreader yew, canoe birch, sugar maple, lilac bushes, and Norway pine flourish elsewhere on the grounds — in all, $25,000 worth of trees, shrubs, and wildflowers donated for landscaping. ◆

— from the Minneapolis Star, Dec. 13, 1968

Klub *(Potato Dumplings)*

1/4	pound salt pork
3	quarts water
4	medium potatoes, shredded
3	cups all-purpose flour
1	teaspoon salt
1	teaspoon baking powder
	flour
	melted butter

Parboil salt pork in water for 40 minutes; remove and cut into small pieces. (Save pork broth.) Combine potatoes, 3 cups flour, salt and baking powder. Shape potato mixture into balls about the size of an apple; press 3 pieces of salt pork into center of each ball. Roll balls lightly in flour; drop into simmering pork broth. Cover and simmer for about 45 minutes or until dumplings are tender. Remove dumplings from broth and serve with melted butter.

10 to 15 dumplings.

Cucumber Salad

1/2	cup cold water
1/2	cup vinegar
3-4	tablespoons vegetable oil
3	tablespoons sugar
1 1/2	tablespoons salt
1/2	teaspoon white pepper
1	teaspoon garlic salt
2	tablespoons dill weed
1	large cucumber, peeled and thinly sliced lettuce

Combine water, vinegar, oil, sugar and seasonings; mix until sugar and salt are dissolved. Add cucumber and refrigerate for at least 1 hour to blend flavors. Serve on lettuce for a salad or as a relish.

3 to 4 salad servings.

State Ceremonial Building

*T*he Minnesota State Constitution prohibits any legislator who votes for an increase in pay for an office from running for that office while a legislator.

Legislators feared that the Irvine house at 1006 Summit Avenue, originally to be an official residence for the governor, might be considered an addition to salary. So they reworded the 1965 bill accepting the Irvines' gift to say that the residence would be for "official public use and ceremonial state functions."

The governor's residing at the former Irvine home was termed "incidental . . . because the official use and ceremonial functions that will be carried on in such a building are essential to the proper function of the chief executive. . . ." [Laws 1965, c684] ◆

Lamb and Cabbage

2   **pounds lamb or mutton, cut into strips**
    water to cover
1   **large cabbage**
6-7 **tablespoons flour**
    salt
    peppercorns

In large skillet or Dutch oven, parboil meat gently for 20 to 25 minutes; drain and reserve broth. Remove meat; set aside. Cut cabbage into thick slices. Place one third of cabbage, then one third of meat in the same pot. Sprinkle with 2 tablespoons of flour, then salt and pepper. Repeat layers; add reserved broth to fill pot half full; cover. Boil briskly for 30 minutes; reduce heat and simmer for 1 to 1¹/₂ hours, stirring occasionally to prevent sticking.

4 to 6 servings.

Serve with boiled potatoes.

Cheese Soufflé

¹/₄ **cup butter**
¹/₄ **cup flour**
¹/₂ **teaspoon salt**
1   **cup milk**
8   **ounces sharp Cheddar cheese, finely shredded**
4   **eggs, separated**

Preheat oven to 300 degrees. In heavy saucepan or double boiler over hot water, melt butter; stir in flour and salt. When blended, add milk and cheese; cook and stir until thick. Beat egg yolks; stir small amount of sauce into yolks. Add yolks to pan of remaining sauce. Turn off heat; cover and let stand on burner or over hot water while beating egg whites until stiff. Fold sauce gently into egg whites until well blended. Pour into ungreased 1¹/₂-quart casserole or soufflé dish and bake in a pan of hot water for 60 to 70 minutes.

4 servings.

Serve with favorite mushroom sauce.

In the Neighborhood

The Horace Hills Irvine family officially deeded their house at 1006 Summit Avenue to the state of Minnesota on August 31, 1965. In September of that same year, the Alice O'Brien Family Foundation of St. Paul donated two adjoining lots to the state.

Pioneer lumberman William O'Brien had purchased the lots in 1905. He sold the property in 1916 to William A. Tilden, whose heirs, in 1948, donated it to St. Luke's Catholic Church across the street.

The O'Briens bought it back to make the gift to the state. O'Brien's grandson, State Representative William J. O'Brien, played a principal role in obtaining the Summit Avenue properties for the state. ◆

— from the St. Paul Dispatch, Sept. 6, 1965

Cold Raspberry Soufflé

4   **teaspoons unflavored gelatin**
3   **tablespoons cold water**
    pinch of salt
2   **packages (10-ounce each) frozen raspberries, thawed**
1   **tablespoon lemon juice**
½   **cup sugar**
3   **egg whites**
1   **cup whipping cream, whipped**
    toasted almonds

In saucepan, soften gelatin in cold water; add salt. Heat slowly and stir to dissolve gelatin. Pureé raspberries in blender. Combine pureé with gelatin, lemon juice and sugar. Place pan over ice water, stirring often until thickened. Beat egg whites until stiff; fold in raspberry mixture, then whipped cream. Spoon into individual dessert dishes. Chill several hours or overnight. Garnish with almonds and additional whipped cream, if desired.

8 to 10 servings.

Note: This recipe uses raw egg whites.

Menu

Luncheon for
Princess Alexandra of England
and
Husband Sir Angus Ogilvy

Sherry

Consommé Madrilène

Chicken Veronique*

Fresh Fruit Salad

Orange-Honey Dressing*

Hot Rum Rolls

Cold Raspberry Soufflé**

*Recipe follows
**See index for recipe

Chicken Veronique

6	large whole chicken breasts, halved, skinned, and boned
6-8	tablespoons butter or margarine
6	tablespoons flour
³/₄	teaspoon salt
¹/₄	teaspoon pepper
2	cups half-and-half
1	cup white wine
	paprika
1	cup seedless green grapes

Brown chicken in 6 tablespoons butter in large skillet. Transfer chicken to shallow casserole. Add more butter to skillet if necessary; blend in flour, salt and pepper and stir until smooth. Stir in half-and-half and wine. Cook and stir until smooth and thick; pour over chicken. Cover and bake at 375 degrees for about 1 hour or until chicken is tender. Sprinkle with paprika; add grapes and bake uncovered for 10 minutes longer.

6 servings.

Orange-Honey Dressing

¹/₃	cup honey
2	tablespoons vinegar
1	tablespoon frozen orange juice concentrate, thawed
1	tablespoon prepared mustard
1	teaspoon salt
³/₄	cup vegetable oil
¹/₄	cup chopped pecans
1	teaspoon poppy seeds

Combine honey, vinegar, orange juice concentrate, mustard and salt. Add oil slowly, beating thoroughly until well blended. Stir in pecans and poppy seeds. Pour into pint jar with tight lid; refrigerate. Shake well before serving.

About 1¹/₂ cups.

An Appreciative Reception

The *St. Paul Pioneer Press*, January 11, 1966, reports on a January 9, 1966 reception at the residence which honored workers and artisans who had put in long hours to ready the house for its first official opening.

The guests included Mr. and Mrs. Charles E. Ludwig of Charles Studio, Minnetonka, who, with only six helpers, made all the drapes for the home in 11 days, using about 800 yards of fabric.

According to Mrs. Ludwig, "My husband did the measuring and installation. I just sewed for 11 days."

Another guest, painter Fritz Runze, said it was not the first time he'd worked in the house, "Forty years ago, I painted here for the Irvines when they owned the house." ◆

Sauerbraten

1	boneless beef rump roast (3 to 4 pounds)
1	tablespoon salt
1/2	teaspoon pepper
2	cups red wine vinegar
4	cups water
2	medium onions, sliced
1	carrot, sliced
1	stalk celery, chopped
4	whole cloves
4	peppercorns
2	bay leaves
2	tablespoons beef suet or shortening
6	tablespoons butter or margarine
5	tablespoons flour
1	tablespoon sugar
10	gingersnaps, crushed

Three to four days before serving, season meat with salt and pepper; place in large non-metallic bowl. Combine vinegar, water, onions, carrot, celery, cloves, peppercorns and bay leaves; pour over meat. Cover and refrigerate for 3 days, turning once a day. To cook, melt suet and 1 tablespoon butter in Dutch oven; brown meat well on all sides. Strain marinade and add to meat. Cover and heat to boiling; reduce heat and simmer until meat is tender, about 3 hours. Remove meat; cool about 15 minutes and slice. Melt remaining butter in small skillet; stir in flour until smooth. Add sugar and cook until quite brown. Stir sugar mixture and gingersnaps into meat liquid. Cook over low heat, stirring constantly until thickened. Return meat to gravy and heat thoroughly. (This can be done early in the day and reheated.) Serve with sweet-sour red cabbage and potato pancakes.

6 to 8 servings.

Menu

Luncheon for
His Excellency Charles Lucet
Ambassador from France

White Wine

Baked Salmon*

Wild Rice

Asparagus with Hollandaise Sauce

Hard Water Rolls

Vanilla Ice Cream with Chocolate Sauce*

Brownies

*Recipe follows

Baked Salmon

2	salmon steaks
$1/3$	cup butter or margarine
$1/2$	teaspoon salt
$1/4$	teaspoon paprika
1	tablespoon Worcestershire sauce
2	tablespoons minced onion

Heat oven to 425 degrees. Place salmon steaks in greased shallow baking dish. Melt butter and add seasonings. Pour over salmon, making sure that some onion goes on each steak. Bake for 30 minutes.

2 servings.

Chocolate Sauce

3	tablespoons butter
2	tablespoons light corn syrup
1	ounce unsweetened chocolate
6	tablespoons whipping cream
1	cup powdered sugar
1	teaspoon vanilla

Heat butter, corn syrup and chocolate in double boiler. Add cream and powdered sugar. Stir until smooth; blend in vanilla.

Makes $1^{1}/_{2}$ cups.

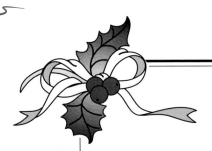

Menu

Christmas Eve
with Governor and Mrs. LeVander

Ost (cheese)

Inlagd Sill (pickled herring)   Knackebröd (Rye Krisp)

Smor (drawn butter)

Lutefisk with Mjolk Säs (milk sauce)

Senap Säs (mustard sauce)   Potatis (potato)

Köttbullar* (Swedish meatballs)

Korv (sausage)   Sylte (head cheese)

Bruna Bönor (brown beans)

Rotos (rutabagas)

Inlagd Rödbetor (pickled beets)

Ragbröd (rye bread)

Risgrynsgröt (rice pudding)   Lingonberry Sauce

Kakor (cookies)

Kaffe (coffee)

Glögg

*Recipe follows

*K*öttbullar *(Swedish Meatballs)*

¹/₃ **cup chopped onion**
1   **tablespoon shortening**
1   **pound ground beef**
¹/₄ **pound ground pork**
¹/₂ **cup cracker crumbs**
¹/₂ **cup milk**
1   **teaspoon cornstarch**
1   **egg, slightly beaten**
1   **tablespoon sugar**
1   **teaspoon salt**
¹/₄ **teaspoon ground nutmeg**
     chopped fresh parsley
3-4 **tablespoons flour**
3   **cups water**
3   **teaspoons instant or 3 cubes**
     beef-flavor bouillon
1¹/₂ **tablespoons lemon juice**
3   **bay leaves**

Cook onion in shortening until tender; combine with meat. Combine crumbs, milk and cornstarch; add to meat mixture. Add egg, sugar, salt, nutmeg and parsley; mix lightly. Refrigerate about 1 hour, then shape into 1-inch balls. Brown in oven-proof skillet; remove meatballs. Stir flour into pan drippings; cook over low heat, stirring constantly until smooth and bubbly, about 1 minute. Remove from heat and stir in water, bouillon, lemon juice and bay leaves. Heat to boiling; boil and stir 1 minute. Return meatballs to skillet and bake at 300 degrees for 1 hour. Remove bay leaves.

6 servings.

Governor Wendell Anderson and First Lady Mary with daughters Amy and Beth and son Brett

The bridge
between
turbulence & affluence

"… Minnesota nurtures
an extraordinary, successful society."

Time Magazine

The '70s, the decade when the country celebrated its 200th birthday, spanned the era from the turbulent '60s to the affluent '80s. The energy crisis passed. Long lines at gas stations and truckers blocking highways in protest of high fuel costs and reduced speed limits disappeared. Minnesota blossomed, and the nation took notice.

When the August 13, 1973, issue of *Time* magazine hit the newsstands, an estimated 4.25 million American households got the good news about the land of sky blue waters. The magazine carried a photo of Governor Wendell Anderson displaying a walleye catch. The headline declared, "MINNESOTA: A State That

The '70s

Governor and First Lady Anderson breakfast with their children in the former third floor servant's bedroom which was converted into a kitchen for the young family.

First ladies found Beaux Arts architecture, history fascinating

Works." The inside feature, "The Good Life In Minnesota," noted that the state had become one of the leading "brain-industry" centers in the nation (in '73, the state had more than 170 businesses in electronics and technical fields). It went on to say, "By a combination of political and cultural tradition, geography, and sheer luck, Minnesota nurtures an extraordinary, successful society."

North Star shines

The *Time* article and the popular "Mary Tyler Moore Show," with its fictional Twin Cities television reporter, Mary Richards, put Minnesota in the national limelight. The election of Minnesota's Senator Walter Mondale to the vice presidency would keep it there.

What the country saw was a state that had grown to include a major metro area boasting more than two million urban dwellers and several newly incorporated businesses such as Cray Research, Inc. (1972), St. Jude Medical, Inc. (1976), and Fingerhut, Inc. (1978). Minnesota's own Harry J. Blackmun had become a Supreme Court Justice in 1970. In sports, the Minnesota Vikings made it to four Super Bowls ('70, '74, '75, and '77). Minnesota women were excited about Billie Jean King's landmark

victory as the first woman to win $100,000 in one year in 1971 and about her defeat of Bobby Riggs on a nationally televised "Battle of the Sexes." Also, in 1974, Little League Baseball, Inc. allowed girls to play, ending the battle over girls playing "boys" sports.

Two governors share a term

Governor Wendell Anderson, First Lady Mary Anderson, and their children were Minnesota's first family from 1970 until 1976. In '76, Minnesota's Senator Walter Mondale became the country's vice president and Anderson replaced him in the Senate. Lieutenant Governor Rudy Perpich then became governor and completed Anderson's second term.

The new governor and his wife Lola wanted their two children to finish high school in their hometown of Hibbing. So the governor moved into the residence alone, and Lola Perpich commuted between St. Paul and Hibbing.

Both first ladies found the residence's Beaux Arts architecture and historical significance fascinating. Mary Anderson turned a room at the top of the stairs into a mini museum with historical photos of 1006 Summit Avenue and of furniture the original owners, the Irvine family, had

The solarium, as decorated in the early '70s, featured a large Star of the North area rug.

Changes clearly distinguish private areas from public areas

contributed. Later, Lola Perpich became an advocate for historic preservation of the house and opened it to the first regular public tours.

The Perpiches dedicated a barrier-free ramp in 1978 to provide access to the residence for people with physical challenges. And they formed an oversight committee to study needs of the residence and make recommendations about its preservation and interior design. During the Perpich years, the residence became an historic site on St. Paul's Historic Sites Register for the Heritage Preservation Commission.

Separating public from private

Because the LeVanders, who preceded them at the residence, had redecorated, the Andersons made only changes necessary to accommodate their young family. The changes, however, would permanently and clearly distinguish private areas from public areas in the house.

"No one could have a clean house for ceremonial use with three young children and two dogs in it, so we went up to the third floor," says Mary Anderson.

The Andersons partitioned off a master bedroom on the second floor, made the open attic into a playroom and the former staff chambers on the third floor into a kitchen with a dining area. For safety's sake they added a plexiglas covering under the staircase railing to prevent eager small children from falling through the openings there. With installation of a security system, guards became a part of the residence scene, to the delight of the Anderson children. "My kids had a great time with the guards. They'd sneak down and have popcorn with them. The kids thought it was our house," says Mary.

Sandwiches and walleye

Residence Cook Ruth Knutson remembers lots of birthday parties and fancy, small sandwiches for kids. Beth Anderson, who was two years old when her family moved to the residence, recalls sampling her first water-chestnut hors d'oeuvres, but says Ruth's strawberry shortcake was among her favorite childhood treats.

As to adult food preferences, Ruth says the governor "loved" walleye. And both Andersons were fond of Corn Bread Stuffing and French Onion soup.

The residence had many famous visitors in the Anderson's time, among them, the king of Sweden, Princess Margaret, Supreme Court Chief Justice Warren Burger, Vice President Hubert Humphrey, Colonel Charles Lindbergh, John Denver and Mary Tyler Moore.

Mary Sue, Governor Rudy Perpich, Rudy Jr., and First Lady Lola

Overall, the '70s were a time of simple family dining

Mary Anderson cooked all the family meals and had the largest events catered because the residence had only 24 place settings of fine china and silver. As first lady, she made it a priority to obtain more. By the end of the Anderson residency, the house had enough to serve 120. The china was the Lenox pattern that First Lady Florence Rolvaag had selected in the '60s.

Mary Anderson also commissioned the Needlework Guild of Minnesota to cover 16 dining room chairs in Bargello stitch as part of the 1976 bicentennial celebration. The design conceptualizes the state symbols and motto and the aurora borealis. Today, the chairs are a high point of residence tours.

Cold cuts and potato salad

After Governor Rudy Perpich took office in 1976, he, for the most part, lived alone at the residence. Ruth, the cook, often left cold cuts and potato salad for him, because she was usually gone for the evening when he came home. He and Ruth developed a unique communication code: When Ruth put a drawing of a smiling face near home-baked goodies, the governor could snack to his heart's content. A scowling face meant "hands-off," indicating that the food was reserved for a special event.

Even though the first lady had to divide her time between responsibilities at home and obligations at the residence, the Perpiches entertained an impressive list of guests. It included Crown Princess Sonja of Norway, Sweden's Undersecretary of Labor and his wife, a delegation from the People's Republic of China, Sweden's Minister of Foreign Affairs, the Twin Cities Consular Corps, six Midwestern governors, the Vice President of the Socialist Republic of Serbia, and the Ambassador of Yugoslavia and his wife.

The '70s, however, were a time of simple family dining. Budget-and-energy-conscious cooks relied on their crock pots for family dinners and entertained with the popular fondue pot. Food and lifestyle magazines like *Better Homes & Gardens* offered recipes to enhance meals of Kraft Macaroni and Cheese, Spam, and Jello for dessert.

At the residence, when the family had dinner together, some of their favorites were Sarma and Potica, reflecting the governor's Yugoslavian ancestry.

Rudy Perpich left the residence in 1978, but would return as governor in 1982 for an eight-year stay. The children would have finished high school, and the family would come to live in the governor's house. ◆

Menu

Dinner in Honor of His Majesty,
King Carl Gustaf XVI of Sweden

April 8, 1976

Canapés

Glazed Fresh Trout*

Cucumber Sauce

Puffed Crackers

Breast of Pheasant with Cream Gravy*

Minnesota Wild Rice*

Asparagus with Lemon Butter

Molded Cranberry Jelly

Blueberry Muffins

Fresh Strawberries

Crème Brulée

Petits Fours

Coffee

*Recipe follows

Glazed Fresh Trout

1   **whole trout (about 5 pounds)**
        salt and pepper
1¼   **cups white wine**
1¼   **cups chicken broth**
2   **envelopes unflavored gelatin**
½   **cup lemon juice**
        thin lemon slices
        thin cucumber slices
        watercress

Remoulade Sauce:

1   **cup mayonnaise**
1   **tablespoon finely chopped
        dill pickle**
1   **tablespoon chopped capers**
2   **teaspoons Dijon mustard**
1   **teaspoon chopped fresh
        parsley**
½   **teaspoon anchovy paste**
½   **teaspoon dried tarragon**
¼   **teaspoon dried chervil**

Preheat oven to 350 degrees. To prepare Remoulade Sauce, combine all ingredients; stir to blend and refrigerate. Sprinkle fish with salt and pepper. Place fish in center of a large sheet of heavy duty foil on a cookie sheet; turn up sides of foil. Add wine and chicken broth. Top with second piece of foil; crimp both pieces together to make a tight seal around fish (fish may be left flat or curved into a letter "C"). Oven poach fish for 35 to 40 minutes or until firm to the touch. Cool fish in wrapping. Drain 2½ cups poaching liquid into saucepan. Soften gelatin in lemon juice; stir into poaching liquid and heat over low heat until gelatin is dissolved. Refrigerate until syrupy. Strip skin from fish; chill until fish is very cold. Place fish on serving platter and spoon half of gelatin over fish; refrigerate until coating hardens. Spoon remaining gelatin over fish until completely coated; chill. Garnish fish with lemon and cucumber slices; add watercress and serve with *Remoulade Sauce*.

5 main dish servings or 10 to 12 first course servings.

Breast of Pheasant *with Cream Gravy*

1	**pheasant, quartered (may be boned)**
	seasoned flour
1/2	**cup clarified butter**
1/2	**cup all-purpose flour**
1	**quart half-and-half**
	salt
	white pepper

Preheat oven to 350 degrees. Dip pheasant pieces in seasoned flour; brown in clarified butter in large skillet (reserve butter). Place pheasant pieces in baking pan. Add a small amount of water, cover and bake for 45 to 60 minutes or until fork tender. Strain butter through cheesecloth; heat, stirring constantly. Stir in flour and half-and-half; bring to a boil, stirring until thickened. Season with salt and pepper. Pour sauce over pheasant; cover and bake at 300 degrees until thoroughly heated.

2 to 3 servings.

Minnesota Wild Rice

Use chicken or beef stock in place of water.

6	**ounces uncooked wild rice**
4	**cups salted water**
1/2	**cup chopped onion**
1/2	**cup butter or margarine**
1 1/2	**cups sliced mushrooms**

Rinse wild rice thoroughly. Place in heavy saucepan with salted water. Heat to boiling; cover and simmer for 45 to 60 minutes or until tender but not mushy. Drain off excess liquid, if any. Sauté onion in butter until soft; add mushrooms and sauté. Add onions and mushrooms to wild rice. Garnish as desired.

4 to 6 servings.

Swedish Rye Bread

2	packages active dry yeast
1/2	cup warm water (105 to 115 degrees)
1¹/2	cups lukewarm milk
2	tablespoons sugar
1	tablespoon salt
2	tablespoons shortening, melted
1/2	cup molasses
3¹/2	cups all-purpose flour
3¹/4	cups medium rye flour

Dissolve yeast in warm water. Combine warm milk, sugar and salt; stir to dissolve. Beat in shortening, molasses and all-purpose flour. Add yeast mixture to molasses mixture and mix well; stir in rye flour. Turn onto lightly floured surface; knead until smooth. Place in greased bowl; turn greased side up. Cover; let rise in warm place until double, about 1 hour. Punch dough down; divide in half. Shape each half of dough into round loaf. Place loaves in opposite corners of lightly greased cookie sheet. Let rise again until double, about 1¹/2 hours. Heat oven to 350 degrees. Bake for 30 to 35 minutes or until loaf sounds hollow when lightly tapped.

2 loaves.

Menu

Formal Dinner
at the Governor's Residence

November 30, 1971

Canapés

Seafood Molds on Bibb Lettuce

Cucumber Sandwiches

Boned Chicken Breast in Cream with Kumquats

Hominy Soufflé with Melted Butter

Fresh Asparagus with Lemon Strips and Bacon

Baking Powder Biscuits

Strawberry Ice Cream*

Fresh Strawberries

Coconut Balls

Lace Cookies

Coffee

*Recipe follows

Strawberry Ice Cream

6   **cups strawberry purée (made from fresh or frozen berries)**

2   **pints whipping cream**

$^1/_2$ **teaspoon salt**

3   **tablespoons lemon juice**

$^1/_3$-$^1/_2$ **cup sugar**

Combine all ingredients; freeze slowly in 4-quart capacity electric or old-fashioned ice cream freezer. After ice cream is frozen, pack freezer with more ice and salt and let stand 2 to 3 hours to harden.

12 to 15 servings (about 2 quarts).

Pecan Pie

1   **unbaked pie shell (10-inch)**

$1^1/_2$ **cups dark corn syrup**

$1^1/_2$ **cups sugar**

5   **eggs**

3   **tablespoons butter or margarine, melted**

$1^1/_2$ **teaspoons vanilla**

$1^1/_4$ **teaspoons salt**

1   **cup pecan halves**

Preheat oven to 400 degrees. Prepare pie shell. Combine syrup, sugar, eggs, butter, vanilla and salt; stir in pecans. Pour filling into pie shell. Cover edge of crust with 2- to 3-inch strip of foil to prevent excess browning. Bake for 15 minutes; reduce oven temperature to 350 degrees and bake until set, 30 to 35 minutes longer. Remove foil during last 15 minutes of baking.

10-inch pie.

Changing Times

As times change, so does the residence. As early as 1922, the Irvines received a building permit for remodeling – probably to expand the sun room (solarium) and to add a fireplace.

Remodeling in the 1970s converted what was the breakfast room (or servants' dining room) during the Irvine years into space for state patrol security officers. Using camera and motion detectors, security personnel keep watch over all areas of the house and grounds 24 hours a day.

The amusement room where the Irvine children played is also in use today. It boasts a lovely stone fireplace and is a perfect place for showing films and slides as after dinner entertainment, or for keeping track of election results on a large-screen TV.

Another area that has changed over the years is the upstairs space that the architect called an "open attic." The Irvines used it for an occasional dancing class. For some governors' children it was a playroom. Other first families used it as a jogging track. Today, it serves primarily as a storage space; fire regulations prevent using it for large groups because of the narrow stairway access. ◆

Norwegian Meatballs

2	pounds ground beef
2	eggs, slightly beaten
3/4	cup all-purpose flour
1	cup milk
1	teaspoon salt
1/4	teaspoon pepper
1	teaspoon ground nutmeg
1	cup chopped onion
2	cans (10 1/2-ounce each) consommé
2	soup cans water
1	cup milk
1/4	cup flour
2	tablespoons steak sauce

Combine ground beef, eggs, 3/4 cup flour, 1 cup milk, salt, pepper and nutmeg. Shape into 1 1/4-inch meatballs. Brown meatballs in skillet; remove, set aside. Add onion to same skillet and sauté. Add consommé and water; heat to boiling. Add meatballs and simmer for 20 minutes; remove meatballs. Strain broth and thicken with 1 cup milk and 1/4 cup flour; stir in steak sauce. Pour gravy over meatballs.

8 servings.

Can be served as main course or first course appetizer.

111

Cheese Sticks

1   **cup all-purpose flour**
1/2   **teaspoon salt**
1/3   **cup butter or margarine**
1/2   **cup shredded sharp Cheddar cheese**
2   **tablespoons water**
    grated Parmesan cheese
    poppy or sesame seed

Preheat oven to 450 degrees. Combine flour and salt; cut in butter and Cheddar cheese. Sprinkle dough with water; stir with fork and form into a ball. Roll dough out on lightly floured surface into 13 x 10-inch oblong. Cut dough into thirds lengthwise; cut each third into 15 crosswise sticks using pastry wheel. Place sticks on ungreased cookie sheets; sprinkle with Parmesan cheese or poppy or sesame seed. Bake sticks 8 to 10 minutes or until light brown.

45 sticks.

Corn Bread Stuffing *(with oysters)*

2   **medium onions, chopped**
4   **stalks celery, chopped**
1/2   **cup butter or margarine**
2   **cups toasted, cubed white bread**
2   **cups unsweetened coarse corn bread crumbs**
1   **teaspoon seasoned salt**
1   **teaspoon salt**
1   **teaspoon poultry seasoning**
1/2   **teaspoon pepper**
1   **egg, slightly beaten**
1/2-1   **cup chopped oysters, optional**

Sauté onions and celery in butter; add bread cubes, crumbs and seasonings. Add egg, mixing lightly with fork; stir in oysters. Makes sufficient stuffing for 12 pork chops or a 6- to 8-pound bird.

4 cups.

Lobster Thermidor

8	lobster tails, fresh or frozen (8- to 10-ounces each)
¹/₂	cup chopped onion
¹/₂	cup butter
2	cups sliced fresh mushrooms
¹/₂	cup all-purpose flour
1	teaspoon salt
¹/₂	teaspoon paprika
¹/₂	teaspoon pepper
2	cups chicken broth
2	cups cream
2	teaspoons Worcestershire sauce
4	egg yolks, slightly beaten
¹/₄	cup sherry
	grated Parmesan cheese

Cook lobster tails; drain. Remove meat from shells; cut meat into pieces and set aside; reserve shells. Preheat oven to 375 degrees. Sauté onion in butter until tender; add mushrooms and cook for 1 minute. Stir in flour and seasonings; cook and stir over low heat until well mixed. Remove from heat and blend in chicken broth, cream and Worcestershire sauce; heat to boiling; cook and stir 1 minute. Stir half of hot mixture into egg yolks; blend egg mixture into remaining hot mixture. Stir in sherry and lobster. Place shells in baking pan; fill with lobster mixture. Sprinkle with Parmesan cheese. Bake for 8 to 10 minutes or until mixture is thoroughly heated.

8 servings.

Menu

Luncheon in Honor of
His Excellency Petar Kostic
Vice President of Socialist Republic of Serbia

April 6, 1978

Lemon Soup

Fillet of Walleye Pike Almandine*

Parsley Buttered New Potatoes

Asparagus with Sauce Dijonnaise

Popovers

Fresh Fruit Compote

Coffee

*Recipe follows

Fillet of Walleye Pike Almandine

8   fresh walleye fillets
1/4-1/3 cup melted butter
1-1 1/2 cups fine bread crumbs
        salt to taste
        sliced almonds, browned in
        butter

Rinse fillets in cold water; pat dry on paper towels. Dip fillets into melted butter to coat well. Place fillets in baking pan and sprinkle with bread crumbs and salt. Broil in preheated broiler for 7 to 10 minutes or until fish flakes. Serve with almonds.

6 to 8 servings.

French Onion Soup

2   large sweet onions
1   tablespoon butter or
        margarine
1   teaspoon cornstarch
2   cans (10 1/2-ounce each) beef
        consommé
1   tablespoon cognac
        salt
1/2   cup light cream
1   egg yolk, beaten
        Worcestershire sauce
12   slices Swiss cheese
6   slices toasted French bread

Peel and slice onions; separate into rings. Sauté onions in butter until soft and golden. Stir in cornstarch. Dilute consommé as directed on cans; add to onion. Simmer about 10 minutes; add cognac and simmer a little longer. Add salt, cream and egg yolk, stirring constantly. Add several shakes of Worcestershire sauce. Place 1 slice of cheese in each of 6 oven-proof soup bowls or individual casseroles; ladle soup over cheese. Top each bowl with slice of toasted bread and another slice of cheese. Place bowls on cookie sheet; broil until cheese is melted and golden brown.

6 bowls.

Cook Ruth Knutson created Walleye Pike Almandine *for Governor Anderson. The governor had sampled a similar version at a local restaurant and raved about it. Mrs. Anderson treated the staff to lunch at that restaurant so Ruth could order the walleye and recreate it for the governor. Ruth served this recipe countless times during her tenure at the residence.*

115

Ruth Knutson was the first and only full-time cook at the residence between 1971 and 1989. She says she never cooked up a disaster because she was always well organized.

Menu

Ethnic Dinner
January 4, 1978

Wild Rice Soup*
Buttered Crackers
Kruska Salad
Sarma*
Rouladen*
Casserole Roasted Krumpir
Kruv and Putar
Walnut Potica
Apple Strudel*
Cottage Cheese Strudel
Coffee

*Recipe follows

Wild Rice Soup

Soup Stock (recipe follows)
1/4   **cup butter or margarine**
2/3   **cup uncooked wild rice**
2   **tablespoons sliced blanched almonds**
1/2   **cup finely diced onion**
1/2   **cup finely diced carrot**
1/4   **cup finely diced celery**
2   **teaspoons arrowroot (optional)**
2   **cups whipping cream**

Prepare *Soup Stock*. Melt butter in heavy kettle; sauté wild rice, almonds, onion, carrot and celery until onion is soft. Add stock; simmer about 1 1/4 hours. If necessary, thicken with 2 teaspoons of arrowroot dissolved in a small amount of the cream. Stir in the rest of the cream just before serving.

6 to 8 servings.

Soup Stock

2   **duck or chicken carcasses**
1   **smoked ham bone**
1   **medium onion, sliced**
2   **teaspoons Maggi seasoning**
    salt and pepper to taste
1   **bay leaf**
1/4   **celery stalk, chopped**
1 1/4   **quarts water**

Combine all ingredients. Heat to boiling; reduce heat and simmer for about 1 1/2 hours. Strain.

Sarma *(Stuffed Cabbage Leaves)*

1	large head cabbage
2	quarts sauerkraut
1	large onion, chopped
1	tablespoon vegetable oil
1¹/₂	pounds ground pork
1	pound ground ham
¹/₂	pound ground beef
¹/₃	teaspoon minced garlic
1	cup uncooked rice
1	egg
	salt and pepper
	bacon strips

Remove core and outer leaves from cabbage. Cover head of cabbage with boiling water; boil 5 minutes; drain and separate leaves. Rinse sauerkraut and drain. Lightly brown onion in oil; mix with meats, garlic, rice, egg, salt and pepper. Roll a generous portion of meat mixture in each cabbage leaf. When leaves are all filled, shape remaining meat into balls. Cover bottom of large roaster pan with sauerkraut; place cabbage rolls and meat balls on top. If it is necessary to have more than 1 layer of rolls, place layer of sauerkraut between layers. End with a layer of sauerkraut and top with bacon strips. Add cold water to almost cover layers. Cover roaster; bake at 350 degrees for 2 hours.

About 22 sarmas.

Rouladen *(Stuffed Beef Rolls)*

Dill pickles are optional.

8	pieces beef sirloin or round steak, thinly sliced
	salt and pepper
	Dijon mustard
¹/₄	cup minced onion
8	dill pickles, finely chopped
12	slices Canadian bacon, chopped
	flour for dredging
	butter or margarine
1¹/₂	cups beef broth
1	bay leaf
1	medium onion pierced with 2 or 3 whole cloves

Pound steaks until very thin. Season with salt and pepper; spread with mustard. Mix minced onion, pickles and bacon; place 1 tablespoon or more of mixture on each piece of steak. Roll up and secure each piece of beef with 2 or 3 toothpicks. Dredge rolls in flour; melt butter in skillet and brown rolls. Add broth, bay leaf and onion; cover and simmer over low heat for about 1¹/₄ hours. Remove bay leaf before serving.

6 to 8 servings.

Apple Strudel

4-6   **apples, peeled and sliced**

2   **tablespoons ground cinnamon**

¹/₂   **cup raisins**

¹/₂   **cup sliced almonds**

2   **cups sugar**

     juice of 1 lemon

¹/₂   **cup bread crumbs**

¹/₂   **package (8-ounce) filo (phyllo) leaves, thawed**

¹/₂   **cup unsalted butter, melted cinnamon-sugar mixture (optional)**

Preheat oven to 375 degrees. Combine apples, ground cinnamon, raisins and almonds with 1³/₄ cups of the sugar and lemon juice. Add the remaining ¹/₄ cup sugar to bread crumbs in separate bowl. Have a large clean cloth covering table; sprinkle lightly with water. Work fast and carefully; place 1 sheet of dough on cloth and brush with butter. Sprinkle with ¹/₄ of the sugar-crumb mixture. Repeat this, layering 3 more times (4 layers in all). Spread apple mixture in a line along the dough, leaving a 2-inch border on the bottom and a 1-inch border on each side. Roll into a tight loaf by pulling up and forward on the bottom edge of the cloth. Fold dough in at borders and seal all edges with butter. Carefully place loaf on buttered sheet pan with sides to catch juices. Brush with melted butter. Sprinkle top of loaf with cinnamon-sugar mixture. Bake for about 45 minutes or until well browned. Serve hot or cold, with whipped cream or ice cream, if desired.

1 large loaf.

Red Cabbage

Sauce can be thickened by adding 2 tablespoons cornstarch dissolved in a little cold water; heat to boiling, boil and stir 1 minute.

1	**medium head red cabbage**
2-3	**tablespoons bacon drippings**
1	**medium onion, chopped**
2	**apples, peeled and sliced**
1	**teaspoon salt**
1/4	**teaspoon pepper**
1/2	**cup sugar**
1/2	**cup vinegar**
1/4-1/2	**teaspoon ground cloves**
1 1/2	**cups water**

Remove outer leaves and rinse cabbage; core and shred. Melt bacon drippings in large skillet; remove from heat; add cabbage and remaining ingredients. Cover and simmer for 1 hour. Taste and adjust seasonings, depending on size of cabbage. Simmer 30 minutes longer.

10 to 12 servings.

Mrs. Anderson's Casserole
with Veal & Pork

3/4	**pound veal cubes**
3/4	**pound pork cubes**
1-3	**tablespoons vegetable oil**
1	**small green pepper, chopped**
5	**stalks celery, chopped**
1	**onion, chopped**
1	**cup macaroni shells, cooked and drained**
1	**can (10 3/4-ounce) cream of mushroom soup**
1	**can (10 3/4-ounce) cream of chicken soup**
1	**can (4-ounce) button mushrooms, drained**
	salt and pepper

Brown veal and pork in oil. Add green pepper, celery and onion; brown lightly. Add macaroni, soups and mushrooms; season with salt and pepper. Bake at 325 degrees for 1 hour; uncover and continue baking for 30 minutes.

6 servings.

Veal Birds

2   **medium onions, chopped**
$^1/_4$ **cup butter or margarine**
6   **slices bread**
      salt and pepper
      dried basil
1   **clove garlic, crushed**
1   **cup finely chopped celery**
8-12 boneless veal cutlets
$^1/_4$ **cup butter or margarine**
4   **ounces fresh mushrooms, sliced**
1   **medium onion, chopped**
2   **teaspoons instant or 2 cubes chicken-flavor bouillon**
2   **cups water**
$^1/_4$ **cup sherry**
      flour

Cook and stir 2 chopped onions in $^1/_4$ cup butter until browned. Crumble bread by rubbing over grater; add to onions. Add salt, pepper, basil, garlic and celery; toss lightly to make stuffing, adding more butter if necessary. Pound cutlets until very thin; top each with stuffing and roll up. Hold each cutlet together with a skewer or tie with string. Melt $^1/_4$ cup butter in large skillet; brown rolls well and remove from skillet. Add mushrooms and 1 chopped onion; sauté. Add flour when mushrooms are brown; stir in bouillon, water and sherry. Return veal to skillet and cook slowly over low heat until tender, about 1 hour. Serve with gravy.

8 to 12 servings.

Veal was a Perpich favorite main dish.

Pineapple Split

1   **package (12-ounce) vanilla wafers, crushed**

$^{1}/_{2}$ **cup butter or margarine, softened**

1   **package (8-ounce) cream cheese, softened**

$^{1}/_{4}$ **cup butter or margarine, softened**

1   **can (20-ounce) crushed pineapple, well drained**

$^{1}/_{4}$ **cup butter or margarine, softened**

2   **cups powdered sugar**

$^{1}/_{2}$ **cup semi-sweet chocolate chips**

$1^{1}/_{2}$ **cups evaporated milk**

2   **large or 3 small bananas**

2   **tablespoons orange or lemon juice**

1   **cup whipping cream, whipped**

1   **jar (3-ounce) maraschino cherries, drained**

$^{1}/_{2}$ **cup coarsely chopped pecans**

Combine crumbs and $^{1}/_{2}$ cup butter. Press on bottom of 13 x 9 x 2-inch pan. Combine cream cheese and $^{1}/_{2}$ cup butter; blend well. Stir in two-thirds of the pineapple (about 1 cup); spread mixture over crust. Combine $^{1}/_{2}$ cup butter, powdered sugar, chocolate chips and evaporated milk in medium saucepan. Cook over medium heat, stirring constantly, until thick and smooth; cool. Slice bananas into $^{1}/_{2}$-inch pieces; drizzle with orange juice and drain well. Arrange banana slices over pineapple-cream cheese layer. Top with cooled chocolate sauce; spread with whipped cream. Sprinkle with remaining pineapple, pecans and cherries. Chill thoroughly before serving.

12 to 15 servings.

$\mathscr{R}$*uth's Cheesecake*

Crust:

1   **cup all-purpose flour**
$^1/_4$ **cup sugar**
1   **teaspoon grated lemon peel**
$^1/_2$ **teaspoon vanilla**
1   **egg yolk**
6   **tablespoons butter or margarine, softened**

Filling:

5   **packages (8-ounce each) cream cheese, softened**
$1^3/_4$ **cups sugar**
2   **tablespoons cornstarch**
$1^1/_2$ **teaspoons grated lemon peel**
$1^1/_2$ **teaspoons grated orange peel**
$^1/_4$ **teaspoon vanilla**
5   **eggs**
2   **egg yolks**
$^1/_4$ **cup whipping cream**
$^3/_4$ **cup dairy sour cream**

To make crust, combine flour, sugar, lemon peel and vanilla. Make a well in center of flour mixture; add egg yolk and butter. Mix with fingertips until dough cleans side of bowl; form into ball. Wrap in plastic wrap or waxed paper; refrigerate 1 hour. Preheat oven to 400 degrees. Grease bottom and side of 9-inch springform pan. Remove side from pan. Roll $^1/_3$ of dough on bottom of pan; trim edge of dough. Bake 8 to 10 minutes or until golden. Meanwhile, divide remaining dough into 3 parts, rolling each part into a strip $2^1/_2$ inches wide and 10 inches long. Assemble springform pan with baked crust on bottom. Fit dough strips to side of pan, joining ends to line inside completely; refrigerate until ready to fill. Preheat oven to 500 degrees.

To make filling, combine cream cheese, sugar, cornstarch, lemon peel, orange peel and vanilla in large mixer bowl. Beat at high speed just to blend. Beat in eggs and egg yolks, one at a time. Add whipping cream and sour cream, beating just until well combined. Pour mixture into crust-lined springform pan. Bake for 10 minutes; reduce oven temperature to 250 degrees and bake for 70 to 80 minutes longer. Cool cheesecake in pan; refrigerate for 3 hours. To serve, loosen pastry from side of pan with spatula; remove side of springform pan.

16 to 20 servings.

Governor Al Quie and First Lady Gretchen Quie with children and grandchildren

A time of coming together

"It's a once in a lifetime thing.
So here I am."

woman in the crowd waiting for the Gorbachevs

*T*he '80s began on a joyous note when, in 1981, 52 Iranian hostages came home to ticker tape parades and yellow ribbons waving from tree branches, bridges, and buildings. The country was in a recession, but the economy improved. As the stock market soared, the '80s became a decade of opulence. The Cold War ended, and despite unrest in many parts of the world, hope for peace came alive.

Caught up in a growing economy, the country was enthralled with the super-rich who came into homes weekly via the popular television series "Falcon Crest" and "Dallas." The White House took on a regal air that set the tone for

The '80s

Each Christmas, Gretchen Quie decorated the house around a central theme. Her favorite year was 1981 when the Kugler musical instrument museum loaned this antique harp along with a music box on legs, horns, flutes, and lutes.

Candlelight dinners drew an unusual mix of people

the times when the country's First Lady Nancy Reagan purchased china at the cost of $920 per place setting.

In contrast, at the Minnesota Governor's Residence, First Lady Gretchen Quie, an artist and potter, held a competition for Minnesota artists, from whom she purchased 12 place settings of hand-thrown stoneware and hand-woven linens. "I wanted casual dishes for small luncheons in the solarium, or for times when a group of friends would join me in my third-floor studio," she said.

Open house

Governor Al Quie, First Lady Gretchen, and their teenage son Ben gladly stepped in out of the fierce cold on the January day they moved into 1006 Summit in 1979. From the start, Gretchen, like others before her, pondered how to make an official state house feel like home, how to make it hospitable to both large and small groups of people she would entertain, and since it was the governor's official residence, how to make it an open and welcoming house for the people of the state.

She and the governor decided on an unusual way to begin sharing the house with Minnesotans. They held a series of drawings and selected individuals to win a tour, a candlelight dinner with the Quies, and an overnight at the residence. Each contest targeted people with unique qualifications — people who worked on Christmas Day, or Salvation Army bell ringers, or unpublished authors. Gretchen particularly remembers a selection that called for someone who lived in a haunted house. When the winner came, she told bewitching after-dinner stories in the darkened dining room.

Tradition and diversity

The governor's inaugural dinner signaled the Quies' dedication to their Scandinavian ancestry with a menu of Swedish Limpa Bread, Swedish Meatballs in Parsleyed Cream Sauce, Fillet of Herring in Wine Sauce, Hungarian Ham with Albert Sauce, and Meringue Tarts. But their respect for tradition also carried over into other cultures.

They hosted three legislative receptions that celebrated local cultural

Cook Ruth Knutson in the residence kitchen

First Lady Gretchen Quie and Governor Al Quie were dairy farmers before he entered politics, and they owned a small farm named "GODSEND" near Marine on the St. Croix. During June Dairy Month in 1980, Gretchen challenged Vikings player Paul Kraus to a milking contest. "We sat on opposite sides of the cow and began to milk her," said Gretchen. "To my surprise, he won the contest."

"Living in the Governor's Residence is … like living over the store."

diversity with ethnic decorations, music, and food such as Indian Fry Bread, Barbecued Chicken Wings, Guacamole, and Vietnamese Egg Rolls. They also rented the apartment over the garage to a family of Vietnamese boat people who became American citizens. That family still visits their host family at the Quie home in Minnetonka, Minnesota.

In a return to their heritage, the Quies ended their time at the residence with parties for King Olav of Norway and King Carl Gustav and Queen Silvia of Sweden as part of the "Scandinavia Today" celebration in 1982.

Fundraising, refurbishing

In 1983, Gretchen told a writer from *Twin Cities Magazine*, "Living in the Governor's Residence is a bit like living over the store." But despite that observation, she had put her energies into making the residence both a comfortable home and state house.

Fifteen years had passed since the house had become the Governor's Residence, and it needed redecorating when the Quies moved in. Gretchen began raising funds for basic refurbishing with the help of a five-member volunteer committee. In August of 1980 her ad hoc committee turned into the governor-appointed 14-member Governor's State Ceremonial Building Council. The council has continued under every governor since 1980, managing fundraising and restoration for the residence.

First Lady Gretchen also formed the 1006 Summit Avenue Society, a volunteer fundraising group. Her talents and those of that group successfully launched the cookbook, *The Governors' Table*, which helped pay for renovating second-floor bedrooms as guest rooms.

After she left the 1006 Summit house, Gretchen said, "Once we moved in and got settled, the Governor's Residence became a wonderful home to enjoy. The best part was opening it up to the public. I cannot tell you how wonderful it is to see the thrilled look on people's faces as they enter this beautiful home."

A presidential visit

The visit of Russian President Mikhail Gorbachev and Raisa Gorbachev on June 3, 1990, was the highlight of Governor Rudy Perpich and First Lady Lola's second stay at the residence. Three years had passed since President Reagan and Gorbachev signed the treaty eliminating intermediate nuclear weapons from Europe. The Berlin Wall had crumbled and Gorbachev announced his plans

Soviet President Mikhail Gorbachev greets First Lady Lola and Governor Rudy Perpich at the residence prior to lunch.

The long, cold war ends and hope for lasting peace arrives

for a whirlwind visit to the United States, which, at the invitation of Rudy Perpich, included Minnesota.

In preparation, St. Paul erected Russian language road signs and planted 260,000 flowering petunias and marigolds along the freeway. Residence Chefs Nathan Cardarelle and Kenneth Grogg, with Goodfellows caterers, planned and replanned the menu for "the lunch of the decade," featuring Minnesota specialties of Pecan-Breaded Walleye, Veal Medallions with Minnesota Morel Sauce, Wild Rice Compote, and Fresh Berries with Minted Sweet Biscuits. Dayton's stores furnished especially designed china, crystal, and linens.

When the day arrived, crowds waited outside the residence, ready to wave and cheer as they had all along the route of the Soviet leader's 45-car entourage. And though it was a wet, cold day for June, people seemed not to notice. A woman in the throng near the State Capitol summed up the feelings of many: "It's a once in a lifetime thing, so here I am."

Heavy renovation

The Perpiches lived with the upheaval of renovation which was part of the architectural master plan for the residence. The extensive work included redoing the carriage house as office space for residence staff; repairing and waterproofing a foundation wall; installing handicapped accessible lavatories in the lower level public areas; remodeling lower level rooms into a family room, reception area, coat room, and conference room; and constructing a terrace around the south side of the residence.

The first lady turned to the restoration projects with an enthusiasm that got results and won her an award from the Minnesota Society of Architects. She held the first benefit for the residence, advertised as a feast for the eyes.

During the "American Craft Expo '87," guests strolled amid the nation's best arts and crafts in a 1911 Summit Avenue decor and enjoyed foods of their choice from 22 tables of elegant appetizers, entrees and salads, including Shrimp and Chicken Wontons, Veal-Duck-Mushroom Paté, Wild Rice Spring Salad, artistic and Scandinavian desserts, and miniature French pastries.

Profits from a cookbook of 150 Minnesota wild rice recipes, *Wild Rice, Star of the North*, went to benefit the residence. And a plan Lola devised for local businesses to "adopt" a room and finance its restoration worked so beautifully that she said, "Design and furnishings of the house are being integrated in a way that they have not since this was the Irvine family home." ◆

Menu

Night
at the Mansion

Sherry

Cider

Hot Cracker Topper*

Chicken Gretchen's Way*

White and Wild Rice

First Lady Spinach Salad

Frozen Strawberry Velvet

* Recipe follows

Chicken Gretchen's Way

1	bunch fresh broccoli
1	broiler-fryer chicken, cut up
1/4	cup chopped onion
1	clove garlic, minced
	butter
1	can (16-ounce) peach halves, drained
	salt and pepper
3/4	cup dairy sour cream
3/4	cup mayonnaise
1/3	cup Parmesan cheese, grated

Remove tough stalks from broccoli. Cut tender stalks and flowerettes into large pieces; steam until crisp-tender, about 3 to 5 minutes. Sauté onion and garlic in 2 tablespoons butter in large skillet until onion is soft. Add chicken pieces and brown, adding more butter as needed until all chicken is browned. Preheat oven to 375 degrees. Place the chicken in a 13 x 9 x 2-inch casserole; cover with foil, bake for 30 minutes. Remove from oven; arrange broccoli and peach halves in pan with chicken. Sprinkle with salt and pepper. Mix sour cream and mayonnaise; spread over chicken, broccoli and peaches. Sprinkle with Parmesan cheese. Bake for 8 to 10 minutes. Do not overbake or sauce will curdle.

6 servings.

Hot Cracker Topper

1	cup pecans, chopped
1/4	cup butter
1	package (8-ounce) cream cheese, softened
2	tablespoons milk
1/2	cup dairy sour cream
2 1/2	ounces dried beef, finely chopped
1/2	green bell pepper, finely chopped
2-3	green onions, finely chopped
1/4	teaspoon pepper
	garlic salt

Toast pecans in butter in small skillet. Preheat oven to 350 degrees. Whip cream cheese, milk and sour cream together. Mix in remaining ingredients except crackers. Spread cheese mixture in flat oven-proof serving dish; top with pecans. Bake for about 20 minutes. Serve with crackers.

10 to 12 servings.

Menu

Constitutional
Officers Dinner

Mushroom Croustades*

Vegetable Dip

Grapefruit, Avocado and Artichoke Salad

Chicken Breasts Fromage*

White and Wild Rice

Spinach-Filled Tomatoes

Poppy Seed Rolls

Crêpes Elaine*

*Recipe follows

Mushroom Croustades

2   **tablespoons butter, softened**

18   **slices fresh white bread, thinly sliced**

4   **tablespoons butter**

3   **tablespoons finely chopped shallots**

$^1/_2$ **pound fresh mushrooms, finely chopped**

2   **tablespoons flour**

$^3/_4$ **cup whipping cream**

$^1/_2$ **teaspoon salt**

$^1/_8$ **teaspoon cayenne pepper**

$1^1/_2$ **tablespoons finely chopped fresh parsley**

1   **tablespoon lemon juice grated Parmesan cheese**

Preheat oven to 400 degrees. Using 2 tablespoons butter, grease bottoms and sides of 18 muffin cups (2-inch). Cut a 3-inch round from each bread slice; fit carefully into muffin cups. Bake 10 minutes or until edges begin to brown. Remove croustades from tins and cool (they can be frozen). Melt 4 tablespoons butter or margarine in heavy skillet; add shallots and stir over moderate heat for 4 minutes. Add mushrooms and stir occasionally; cook until moisture has evaporated, for 10 to 15 minutes. Remove skillet from heat; thoroughly stir in flour. Return skillet to heat; add whipping cream, stirring until it boils. When thickened, remove from heat and stir in seasonings and lemon juice; cool. Just before serving, heat oven to 350 degrees. Fill croustades with mushroom mixture; sprinkle with Parmesan cheese. Bake about 5 minutes or until bubbly.

18 appetizers.

Chicken Breasts Fromage

8   chicken breasts (7- to 8-ounces each), halved, skinned and boned

2   tablespoons butter

$1/2$ pound fresh mushrooms, sliced

$2/3$ cup (about 3 ounces) shredded boiled ham

1   tablespoon dry sherry

1   teaspoon lemon juice

1   teaspoon fresh or $1/2$ teaspoon dried tarragon

1   small clove garlic, minced

2   cups shredded Swiss cheese

     salt and freshly ground pepper

     flour

$1/4$ cup butter

2   tablespoons cognac or brandy

1   teaspoon tomato paste

1   teaspoon Dijon mustard

3   tablespoons flour

$1^1/4$ cups chicken broth (preferably homemade)

1   cup whipping cream

2   tablespoons dry white wine

1   tablespoon dry sherry

$1/2$ teaspoon white pepper

$1/2$ cup shredded Gruyère cheese

     parsley sprigs

     cherry tomatoes

Cut a pocket in the thickest side of each chicken breast. Melt 2 tablespoons butter over medium heat and sauté mushrooms for 3 to 4 minutes. Stir in ham, sherry, lemon juice, tarragon and garlic. Cook 1 minute; remove from heat and add Swiss cheese, salt and pepper to taste. Stuff heaping tablespoonful of mixture into each breast. Place on cookie sheet and cover with waxed paper. Place another cookie sheet on top and weight down with cans. Refrigerate for a few hours. Coat chicken with flour. Melt $1/4$ cup butter in skillet and brown chicken breasts. Warm cognac and flame chicken. Place chicken in buttered baking pan.

Preheat oven to 350 degrees. Stir tomato paste and mustard into skillet. Mix 3 tablespoons flour with small amount of chicken broth until smooth. Stir in remaining broth; add to skillet and simmer, stirring until slightly thickened. Gradually add cream, wine, sherry and white pepper. Pour over chicken and bake for 20 to 30 minutes. Sprinkle chicken with Gruyère cheese and return to oven to melt cheese. Serve with parsley and tomato garnish.

8 servings.

Crêpes Elaine

2¼ cups all-purpose flour

1½ tablespoons sugar

¾ teaspoon baking powder

¾ teaspoon salt

3 cups milk

3 eggs

3 tablespoons butter or margarine, melted

¾ teaspoon vanilla

10 sticks of vanilla ice cream, sized to roll into crêpes

whipped cream

toasted almonds or pistachio nuts

Combine flour, sugar, baking powder and salt; stir in remaining ingredients. Beat with rotary beater until smooth. Lightly butter 6- to 8-inch skillet; heat over medium heat until bubbly. Pour scant ¼ cup of batter into skillet; quickly rotate until film of batter covers bottom. Cook until lightly browned; loosen with spatula and turn. Cook other side until lightly browned. Stack crêpes with waxed paper between; keep covered. Prepare Chocolate-Orange Sauce. Roll sticks of ice cream in crêpes and place 2 on each dessert plate. Serve with Chocolate-Orange Sauce; garnish with whipped cream and nuts.

5 servings

Chocolate-Orange Sauce

¼ cup butter

1¾ cups brown sugar, packed

4 ounces semi-sweet chocolate, chopped

2 ounces unsweetened chocolate

⅓ cup orange juice

½ cup creme de cocoa

¼ cup white rum

Melt butter, brown sugar and chocolate over medium heat. Add orange juice and bring to a boil; stir in creme de cocoa. Add rum and flame; after flame goes out, serve hot over crêpes.

137

Menu

Pottery
Dinner

Spinach-Stuffed Chicken

Wild Rice Pilaf*

Green Beans Potomac

Anadama Bread*

Blitzen Torte*

*Recipe follows

Anadama Bread

¹/₂   **cup yellow corn meal**
2   **cups boiling water**
¹/₂   **cup molasses**
2   **teaspoons salt**
1   **tablespoon butter**
1   **package active dry yeast**
¹/₂   **cup warm water (105 to 115 degrees)**
4¹/₂-6¹/₂ cups all-purpose flour

Combine corn meal and boiling water in large bowl; cool slightly. Add molasses, salt and butter; cool to lukewarm. Dissolve yeast in warm water; add to cornmeal mixture. Add 4¹/₂ cups of the flour; beat until smooth. Cover; let rise in warm place until double, about 1 to 1¹/₂ hours. Stir in enough flour to make dough easy to handle. Knead until smooth, about 5 minutes. Divide dough in half; shape into loaves. Place each loaf into a greased 8¹/₂ x 4¹/₂ x 2¹/₂-inch pan. Let rise until double, about 1 hour. Heat oven to 350 degrees; bake 50 to 60 minutes.

2 loaves.

Wild Rice Pilaf

1   **cup wild rice**
¹/₄   **cup chopped onion**
¹/₄   **cup slivered almonds**
¹/₄   **cup butter**
¹/₂   **cup raisins**
2   **teaspoons instant chicken bouillon**
¹/₄   **teaspoon salt**
³/₄   **teaspoon garlic salt**
1   **tablespoon chopped parsley**
1   **can (4-ounce) mushrooms, drained, optional**
2   **cups water**

Wash rice well. Cook in water to cover for 20 minutes; drain and rinse. Sauté onion and almonds in butter. Combine with rice and remaining ingredients. Bake at 350 degrees for 45 minutes in covered casserole.

6 servings.

Greens & whole grains

The weight-loss mania and health consciousness craze of the late '60s and '70s persisted into the '80s. Diet and exercise books repeatedly made the best seller list. Nutra Sweet appeared on the market, and women laced on their Nikes and walked briskly to work while listening to their Sony Walkmans.

First Lady Gretchen Quie loved her morning jogs along Summit Avenue, and when not entertaining, watched her calorie count. "I asked Ruth Knutson to add more fresh fruits and vegetables and whole grains to our menus, but we couldn't resist Ruth's Fillet of Walleyed Pike, Spinach-Stuffed Chicken, and Brandy Snaps."

Special events, which called for special foods, also featured vegetables and grains. Donna Funk of Gladstone House, a favorite caterer at the residence, developed a Royal Vegetables recipe for the king and queen of Sweden. When Julia Child asked for wild rice recipes from Minnesota, she created a Wild Rice Spring Salad that Lola Perpich ordered for a fundraising event to benefit the residence. ◆

Blitzen Torte

¹/₂ **cup butter, softened**

¹/₂ **cup sugar**

4 **eggs, separated**

3 **tablespoons milk**

³/₄ **cup all-purpose flour**

1 **teaspoon baking powder**

1 **cup sugar**

¹/₂ **cup chopped walnuts**

1 **jar (10-ounce) raspberry or strawberry jam**

1 **cup whipping cream, whipped**

Cream butter and ¹/₂ cup sugar; mix in egg yolks and milk. Combine flour and baking powder; add to creamed mixture. Beat until light and fluffy, about 5 to 8 minutes. Spread into 2 greased 8- or 9-inch round cake pans with circular looseners. Preheat oven to 350 degrees. Beat egg whites until foamy; gradually add 1 cup sugar, beating until stiff and glossy. Spread half of meringue on batter in each pan. Sprinkle 1 layer with walnuts. Bake for 25 minutes or until meringue is set and lightly browned; cool. Carefully remove layers from pans. Place plain layer on plate with meringue down. Spread jam over layer; spread cream over jam. Top with meringue and nut layer, nut side up.

12 servings.

Menu

Canadian Ambassador's Dinner

February 12, 1979

Champagne Punch

Assorted Hors d'Oeuvres

Vichyssoise*

Bread Sticks

Spinach and Bacon Salad*

Walleye Pike with Toasted Almonds

Small Parsleyed Potatoes

Peas in Onion Cups

Crescent Rolls

Peaches Almandine

* Recipe follows

Vichyssoise

6	leeks or 1 large Bermuda onion, finely chopped
2	tablespoons butter
1	stalk celery, chopped
2	medium potatoes, cut up
5	cups chicken stock
	salt and pepper
3/4	cup heavy cream
1	tablespoon chopped chives

In large saucepan, melt butter; add leeks, celery and potatoes. Cover and cook over low heat for 25 to 30 minutes, stirring occasionally. Cook until very soft but not brown. Stir in stock and cook for 12 to 15 minutes; season to taste with salt and pepper. Pureé in food mill, blender or food processor. Stir in cream; taste and adjust seasoning. Refrigerate; sprinkle with chives before serving.

6 servings.

Spinach and Bacon Salad

1 1/2	pounds fresh spinach
3	tablespoons wine vinegar
5	tablespoons peanut oil
5	tablespoons olive oil
2	teaspoons Dijon mustard
1	clove garlic, minced
1/2	cup chopped fresh parsley
	salt and pepper
8	slices bacon, crisply fried and crumbled
1/2	pound fresh mushrooms, sliced
1	hard-cooked egg

Trim off all stems and wash spinach; dry well and tear into bite-sized pieces. Combine vinegar, oils, mustard, garlic, parsley, salt and pepper; mix well. When ready to serve, toss spinach with dressing. Top with bacon and mushrooms. Finely grate or sieve egg for garnish.

6 servings.

Al's Best Doggone Pancakes

If using buttermilk, decrease baking powder to 1¹/₂ teaspoon and add ¹/₂ teaspoon baking soda.

1   **cup milk**
2   **tablespoons vegetable oil**
1   **egg**
1   **cup all-purpose flour**
¹/₂   **teaspoon salt**
2   **tablespoons sugar**
2   **tablespoons baking powder**

Combine milk, oil and egg; beat well. Combine dry ingredients; stir in to make smooth batter. Grease griddle if necessary. Cook pancakes over low heat.

About nine 4-inch pancakes.

German Oven Pancake

¹/₂   **cup flour**
3   **eggs, slightly beaten**
¹/₂   **cup milk**
2   **tablespoons melted butter**
¹/₄   **teaspoon salt**
   lemon wedges
   powdered sugar
   melted butter

Preheat oven to 400 degrees. Gradually add flour to eggs, beating with rotary beater. Stir in milk, butter and salt. Grease 9- or 10-inch heavy skillet. Pour batter in cold skillet; bake for 20 minutes. Loosen with wide spatula; cut into wedges. Serve hot with lemon wedges, powdered sugar and melted butter.

4 servings.

$\mathscr{S}$ummit Cheese Ball

2	packages (8-ounces each) cream cheese, softened
2	ounces blue cheese, crumbled
4	ounces sharp Cheddar cheese, shredded
2	teaspoons grated onion
1/4	teaspoon garlic powder
1/2	teaspoon Worcestershire sauce
1/2	teaspoon seasoned salt
1/2	cup chopped pecans

Beat cheeses together in mixer. Add remaining ingredients except pecans; mix well. Cover and refrigerate several hours or overnight. Shape cheese mixture into a ball; roll in pecans before serving. Serve with a variety of crackers.

12 to 15 servings.

$\mathscr{B}$roccoli *with Browned Butter*

1	large bunch broccoli
1/2	cup butter
3	tablespoons fine dry bread crumbs

Trim and wash broccoli. Cook until crisp-tender; drain. Heat butter over medium heat until browned; cool slightly. Stir in crumbs; sprinkle over cooked broccoli.

8 to 10 servings.

Also good on cauliflower.

145

Court Bouillon

Use to poach salmon, shrimp, or vegetables.

14	cups water
1	cup cider vinegar
1	large onion, finely chopped
2	stalks celery, chopped
2	carrots, chopped
5	parsley sprigs
1	tablespoon salt
1	teaspoon peppercorns, crushed
1/2	teaspoon whole cloves
1	bay leaf
1/2	fresh lemon, thinly sliced

Combine water, vinegar, vegetables, seasonings and lemon slices in large kettle; simmer 30 minutes.

Spinach-Filled Tomatoes

8	large firm tomatoes
	salt
2	packages (10-ounces each) frozen chopped spinach, thawed and thoroughly drained
3/4	cup butter
2	tablespoons minced shallots
1-2	cloves garlic, crushed
2	tablespoons minced parsley
1/2	teaspoon salt
	freshly ground pepper
1	cup grated Parmesan cheese
1/2	cup bread crumbs

Preheat oven to 350 degrees. Cut top third from tomatoes; remove center, leaving some pulp. Sprinkle with salt; fill with spinach. Combine butter, shallots, garlic, parsley, salt and pepper; spread over spinach. Mix cheese and bread crumbs; spread thickly on each tomato. Place in baking pan and bake for 15 to 20 minutes; brown under broiler.

8 servings.

Grandma Quie's Coconut Bars

$^1/_2$ **cup butter, softened**

$^1/_2$ **cup brown sugar, packed**

1   **cup all-purpose flour**

2   **eggs**

1   **cup brown sugar, packed (or half brown and half granulated sugar)**

1   **teaspoon vanilla**

2   **tablespoons flour**

$^1/_2$ **teaspoon baking powder**

$^1/_4$ **teaspoon salt**

$1^1/_2$ **cups flaked coconut**

1   **cup chopped nuts**

Preheat oven to 375 degrees. Combine butter, $^1/_2$ cup brown sugar and 1 cup flour; pat into 13 x 9 x 2-inch pan. Bake for 10 minutes. Beat eggs; add remaining ingredients and mix well. Spread on baked crust and return to oven for 15 minutes. Cool slightly; cut into bars.

2 to $2^1/_2$ dozen bars.

Menu

Perpich
Reception

Gingered Chicken Broth*

West Coast Salad*

Crown Roast of Pork with Red Wine Sauce*

Fruit Dressing*

Broccoli with Red Pepper Garnish

Rolls

Strawberry Crêpes

*Recipe follows

Gingered Chicken Broth

4   **cups chicken broth**
1   **slice fresh ginger root**
1   **tablespoon lemon juice**
     salt to taste
2   **green onions**
2   **small mushrooms**

Heat chicken broth. Add ginger, 1 whole green onion and the white part of the second. Save the green top. Simmer, not hard, for 20 minutes. Add salt and lemon juice to taste; strain. Ladle broth into cups or bowls. Garnish with thin slices of the green onion top and thin slices of mushrooms. Serve hot.

6 to 8 servings.

West Coast Salad

1   **pound small beets, steamed until tender**
1   **package frozen artichoke hearts (9 to 10 ounces)**
1   **head red leaf or Boston lettuce**
1   **avocado**
     Dressing
1   **cup alfalfa sprouts**
$1/2$ **cup minced green onions**

Peel beets and quarter or slice if large. Cool. Cook artichokes in 1 inch salted water until just tender; cool under cold running water and refrigerate. Arrange lettuce on plates. Mound beets, artichokes and avocado in center and pour dressing over top. Circle with sprouts and sprinkle with onions.

6 to 8 servings.

Dressing

9   **tablespoons olive oil**
3   **tablespoons white wine vinegar**
1   **tablespoon Dijon mustard**
$1/2$ **teaspoon minced garlic**
$1/2$ **teaspoon salt**
$1/4$ **teaspoon pepper**

Combine all ingredients in a jar and shake well to blend. Pour over salad.

Crown Roast of Pork

with Red Wine Sauce and Fruit Dressing

Unstuffed roast may be assembled early in the day and refrigerated. Remove from refrigerator 2 hours before cooking. The string of cranberries is an optional garnish, festive for holidays and special gatherings.

Variation: Roast without dressing and fill center of meat with cooked mushrooms and peas or Brussels sprouts just before serving.

lemon juice

1   **crown pork roast (7- to 8-pounds; 12 ribs), all fat removed**

salt and freshly ground pepper

Fruit Dressing

$^1/_2$ **cup Dijon mustard**

2   **tablespoons soy sauce**

2   **garlic cloves, minced**

1   **teaspoon sage**

$^1/_4$ **teaspoon marjoram**

kumquats, fresh or preserved, or paper frills (garnish)

fresh cranberries or grapes strung on heavy thread

Red Wine Sauce

Preheat oven to 325 degrees. Moisten paper towel with lemon juice and rub over roast. Insert meat thermometer into meatiest section of roast, being sure not to touch bone. Place roast on rack in roasting pan and sprinkle with salt and pepper. Cover exposed ends of bones with foil to prevent burning; crumple additional foil and place in center of roast to help retain shape. Roast uncovered 1 hour. While meat is cooking, prepare *Fruit Dressing*. Let stand at room temperature. Combine mustard, soy sauce, garlic, sage and marjoram and baste roast with mixture. Continue cooking 1 hour, basting after 30 minutes with pan juices. Remove foil from center and paint inside of roast with juices. Pack dressing into center of roast. Cover dressing with foil and continue cooking until meat thermometer registers 170 degrees, about 1 to $1^1/_2$ hours more. Remove foil from bone tips and cover each with kumquat or paper frill. Loop cranberries between bones, allowing them to drape around sides of roast. Serve with *Red Wine Sauce* on the side, if desired.

12 servings.

Variations: Substitute crown roast of lamb for pork. If using lamb, substitute 2 teaspoons fresh rosemary for sage in basting mixture. Roast lamb until thermometer reaches 120 degrees, then remove foil from center of meat. Paint inside with basting mixture and fill with dressing. Continue roasting until thermometer reaches 130 to 135 degrees. Garnish as for pork roast.

Fruit Dressing

2	tablespoons butter
2	medium onions, chopped
1	cup chopped celery
3	cups cooked white rice
½	teaspoon marjoram
½	teaspoon thyme
	dash of sage
	salt and freshly ground pepper
2	cans (7-ounce each) pineapple tidbits, drained

Melt butter in large skillet over low heat. Add onion and celery and sauté until onion is golden. Stir in rice, marjoram, thyme, sage and salt and pepper to taste, blending well. Add remaining ingredients and stir to combine.

Fruit Dressing may also be served as a side dish: add 1 cup chicken stock and bake covered 30 minutes or until liquid is completely absorbed. Fluff with fork.

Red Wine Sauce

1½	cups red currant jelly
½	cup ruby port wine
	juice of 2 oranges
2	tablespoons fresh lemon juice
2	tablespoons prepared mustard
2	teaspoons paprika
2	teaspoons fresh grated ginger or 1 teaspoon dried
	grated orange peel

Melt jelly in 1-quart saucepan over low heat. Add wine, orange and lemon juices, mustard, paprika and ginger and simmer a few minutes, stirring occasionally but thoroughly. Grate the orange peel; add and cook 1 minute more.

Makes 2 cups.

Red Wine Sauce may be prepared up to 2 weeks ahead and refrigerated.

151

Spinach Wild Rice Salad

1	cup uncooked wild rice (3 cups cooked)
1/4	cup vegetable oil
2	tablespoons white wine vinegar
2	teaspoons soy sauce
1	teaspoon sugar
1/4	teaspoon ground ginger
2	cups finely torn fresh spinach
1-2	tomatoes, chopped
1	cup sliced cauliflowerets
1/2	cup sliced green onions
1/2	cup crisply fried crumbled bacon

Cook wild rice according to package directions; cool slightly. Combine oil, vinegar, soy sauce, sugar and ginger. Add to warm rice. Cover and refrigerate. Before serving, fold in remaining ingredients.

8 to 10 servings.

Curried Chicken Salad

5	cups cooked chicken, a 4-5 pound chicken, cut for salad
1	cup diced celery
1/2	medium onion, chopped
1 1/2	teaspoons salt
1/8	teaspoon pepper
2	cups pineapple tidbits, well drained
2	cups seedless grapes
1 1/2	cups toasted almonds
1 1/2	cups mayonnaise
1	teaspoon curry
6	hard-boiled eggs
	tomato slices

Combine chicken, celery, onion, salt and pepper. Mix well and chill. Add pineapple, grapes and almonds. Combine mayonnaise and curry; add to chicken-fruit mixture. Garnish with hard-boiled eggs and tomato slices.

10 servings (as main dish).

Shrimp Salad Macadamia a la Vinaigrette

20   **large shrimp, shelled and deveined (tails intact)**
     Court Bouillon **** for poaching (about 6 to 8 cups)**
16   **snow peas**
10   **large white mushrooms, cleaned and thinly sliced**
$^1/_2$ **cup chopped unsalted macadamia nuts**
3   **tablespoons finely minced red onion**
     Vinaigrette
8   **lettuce leaves**

** See index for recipe

Poach shrimp in gently simmering *Court Bouillon* until pink, about 3 minutes. Transfer shrimp to bowl using slotted spoon. Let shrimp cool to room temperature, then refrigerate. Carefully slice 8 largest shrimp in half lengthwise down through tails. Reserve for garnish. Slice remaining shrimp in medallions crosswise, discarding tails. Blanch snow peas in boiling salted water for 2 to 3 minutes. Drain well and pat dry with paper towels. Cut each pod diagonally into 3 pieces. Combine shrimp, snow peas, mushrooms, macadamia nuts and onion in large bowl. Add *Vinaigrette* to taste and toss gently. Arrange lettuce leaves on individual plates. Mound salad in center. Garnish each serving with 2 reserved shrimp halves. Pass any remaining vinaigrette separately.

8 servings.

If preferred, substitute 1 to 1¹/₂ pounds fresh crabmeat for the shrimp.

Vinaigrette

2   **tablespoons Dijon mustard**
$^1/_4$ **cup lime juice or to taste**
2   **tablespoons chopped fresh dill or 2 teaspoons dried dill weed**
$^1/_2$ **cup olive oil**
$^1/_2$ **cup vegetable or corn oil**
     salt and freshly ground pepper

Combine mustard and lime juice in small bowl and mix well. Add chopped dill. Add oils 1 tablespoon at a time, whisking well after each addition. Add more lime juice if desired. Season to taste with salt and pepper.

About 1¹/₂ cups.

Shrimp Creole

If using raw shrimp, cook only until shrimp turns pink. If using cooked shrimp, add just before serving. Serve over rice.

3 tablespoons olive oil

1¹/₂ cups chopped onion

1 cup chopped celery, not too fine

2 garlic cloves, minced

1 cup chopped green pepper, not too fine

1 bay leaf

¹/₂ teaspoon thyme

¹/₂ teaspoon basil

1 tablespoon Worcestershire sauce

1 teaspoon sugar

5 drops Tabasco sauce

salt and pepper to taste

2¹/₂ cups Italian tomatoes

1 can (15-ounce) tomato sauce

¹/₄ cup chopped parsley

1-2 pounds shrimp

rice

Sauté onion, celery and garlic in oil for 3 minutes. Add remaining ingredients except shrimp and simmer for 20 to 30 minutes. Add shrimp; heat and serve.

4 to 6 servings.

Chilled Papaya Bisque

4 papayas

¹/₂ teaspoon salt

¹/₂ cup milk

4 ounces vanilla ice cream

¹/₂ cup lemon-lime soda

4 ounces fresh cream

4 ounces coconut liqueur

mint sprigs

Cut papaya in half lengthwise; remove seeds and meat. Save shells. Place papaya meat in blender and blend until smooth. Add remaining ingredients; mix well and chill. Serve in papaya shells garnished with mint sprigs.

8 servings.

Green and White Chicken

2 tablespoons butter

5-6 boneless chicken breast halves, skinned

salt and freshly ground pepper

2 large shallots or green onions, minced

$^{1}/_{2}$ cup chicken stock or canned low-salt broth

2 cups whipping cream

$1^{1}/_{4}$ cups freshly grated Romano cheese

1 bunch green onions, chopped

$^{3}/_{4}$ pound spinach linguine or fettuccine

2 tablespoons butter, room temperature

freshly grated Romano cheese

Melt 2 tablespoons butter in heavy large skillet over medium-low heat. Season chicken with salt and pepper. Add to skillet and sauté until cooked through, turning occasionally, about 12 minutes. Transfer to heated plate and tent with foil to keep warm. Add shallots to same skillet and stir 1 minute. Add stock, increase heat and boil until reduced to glaze, about 5 minutes. Add cream and boil until slightly thickened, stirring occasionally, about 5 minutes. Add $1^{1}/_{4}$ cups Romano cheese and green onions and stir until cheese melts and sauce thickens, adding juices accumulated on chicken plate. Season generously with pepper. Meanwhile, cook linguine in large pot of rapidly boiling salted water, stirring occasionally to prevent sticking. Drain well. Transfer to large heated bowl. Add 2 tablespoons butter and mix until butter melts. Serve sauce over chicken.

5 to 6 servings.

Jessica Carlson admires the flowers that line the flagstone paths. Children of the Irvines and the governors are: Elizabeth, Thomas, Clotilde, and Olivia Irvine (1911-1965); Kristin and Paul Rolvaag (1965-1966); Dyan, Hap, and Jean LeVander (1967-1970); Amy, Beth, and Brett Anderson (1971-1976); Ben, Fredric, Jennifer, Daniel, and Joel Quie (1979-1982); Mary Sue and Rudy (Jr.) Perpich (1977-78, 1983-1990); and Jessica, Anne, and Tucker Carlson (1990-).

Celebrations

Especially for children

Secret panels, dumbwaiters, and talking gates

The 1006 Summit Avenue house has been home to 15 children, beginning with the Irvines. Most have fond memories of the house and the unusual characteristics of living in a governor's residence.

Olivia Irvine Dodge remembers that her friends were impressed with the secret panel in the dining room. She also remembers visits from Santa, which continue today, and special parties for children.

Ben Quie says, "I was 17 when we moved into the residence in 1979. I didn't want one of the 'fancy' bedrooms on the second floor and found a corner room next to a kitchen on the third floor. It had a 30-foot rope ladder for a fire escape.

Children

The Carlsons invited "Make a Wish" children to their 1993 Easter Brunch. Ben Hummel, a child with a rare disease requiring him to get a lung transplant, wrote to Governor Carlson about how the children in his class at Windom Elementary School raised $1,000 to pay back the Make a Wish Foundation for his trip to Disney World. The Governor invited Ben's whole class to the residence for lunch.

Life at the residence created friendships between children and staff

"It was odd coming home from school and having iron gates swing open to let me in," Ben says. However, he got acquainted with the guards, the state patrol officers who handle security for the first family, and spent hours with them and his friends in the security office.

"I remember the cookies and desserts in the big refrigerator. It was fun when my folks were gone; Ruth (Knutson, the cook) or a guard would call on the intercom and ask if I wanted a plate sent up on the dumbwaiter. Some of my favorite foods were walleye with almonds, Brandy Snaps with ice cream, and Parmesan bread sticks.

"We did some crazy things, too. We pressed our faces on the copy machine in the basement, played miniature golf in the attic 'ballroom' with Mom's golf clubs, and took turns riding up and down on the dumbwaiter."

One of the Quie grandchildren, Andrew Coffin, was delighted with his first visit to the residence. To the two-year-old's amazement, the big iron gates talked back when he spoke to them.

Kiddie cocktails and desserts

"I was two when we moved into the Governor's Residence," says Beth (Elizabeth Ann) Anderson, Governor Wendell Anderson's daughter. "My mother always said the residence was not our house; it belonged to the state, and we should try to behave ourselves when guests were there. That was not easy.

"Whether there were guests or not, we had a ball playing hide and seek throughout the house, or composer on the grand piano in the entryway. We would sometimes get the security guards, staff, or chefs to play with us.

"My most vivid memories of food were bacon and water chestnut hors d'oeuvres, with toothpicks I tried to eat, kiddie cocktails, and Ruth's Strawberry Shortcake. I remember my mother driving the three of us, screaming in the back seat of an enormous green station wagon to the local Fish 'N Chips. We would bring the meal home and eat on the guest porch in the summer."

Mary Sue Bifulk remembers the Pineapple Banana Split Dessert that Ruth made. She says, "It was my favorite. I still dream about it to this day."

Staff at the residence are: (top row) Kenneth Grogg, Chef; Julie Kruse, Horticulturist, Nathan Cardarelle, Chef, (middle row) Barbara Hoffmann, Residence Director; Joyce Pellow, Administrative Assistant; Michelle Albers, Public Relations Assistant, (bottom row) Vicki Score, Housekeeper; and Deb Rhein, Dining Room Supervisor.

Jessica Carlson's 10th birthday party

Holidays at the residence are a time of fun and celebration

With the Carlsons, the Governor's Residence again saw small children and pets after more than a decade. Daughter Jessica and friends built forts in the bushes and propped up Cabbage Patch dolls in the front fence. On the first warm day in 1991, the children ended up in the water fountain.

Jessica first learned to ride her bike in the parking lot. And, it wasn't long before she and friends were a common sight biking in the backyard.

Bunnies and goblins

Holidays are a time of fun and celebration for the Carlsons. An Easter Brunch with the Easter bunny, egg hunt, games, and stories has become an annual tradition. The Carlsons invite children with special needs or serious illnesses.

Goblins, spiders, cobwebs, and ghosts greet young visitors as they come for treats during the Halloween open house. Santa Claus and the first family host an open house with the residence festively decorated for the holidays.

During visits to schools, the Governor and Susan often invite students who do additional reading to the residence for lunch. The menus for these groups vary from hamburgers to pizza, Chicken Fingers to Mostaccioli. Fruit and chocolate chips cookies usually complete the meal. Many students say the best part of their visit is the tour of the tunnel, which connects the residence with the carriage house.

A garden, just for kids

The Children's Garden is a new addition to the Governor's Residence. Susan initiated the project after hearing about the White House Children's Garden. She envisioned a beautiful, serene place to enjoy the grounds and reflect on the memories they hold.

At the dedication ceremony in July 1993, Susan said, "I hope that the garden will remind future governors of the commitment the state has to children." The garden of flower beds and wild flowers surrounds a lily pond and the path that follows the south and east perimeter of the grounds. "It really is glorious," Susan says.

Blazing orange, radiant red, intense

Clown and kids at dedication of the Children's Garden

161

Children came to demonstrate rope-jumping skills when Arnold Schwarzenegger visited.

Garden boasts plants with names that make kids giggle

purple, gleaming yellow, brilliant white, velvety green — a rainbow of colors jumps out to greet those who visit the Children's Garden. The garden boasts balloon flowers, hen and chickens, orange sneeze weed, ostrich fern, rocket ligularia, butterfly weed -- and other plants with names that make children giggle.

Just outside the residence solarium, a flagstone path invites guests to wander past the sparkling water of the lily pond — home to fish and a monkey (really a creeping fig hanging from a nearby tree). Engraved plaques on Minnesota rocks amid the perennials, wildflowers, spring bulbs, and lush hosta, call to mind the children and families who are part of the history of this lovely home. Carved teak benches summon all passersby to stop, sit, relax, and enjoy their surroundings.

And all the while, "Carl," a young boy on a bicycle, sits anxiously waiting to head out across the lawn. The bronze sculpture is by Minnesota artist Douglas Forsberg, who gave it to the residence in 1993.

At the dedication, the 250 guests included Olivia Irvine Dodge, whose family built the house and lived in it until 1965. And, for the first time, children of the governors who served Minnesota since the house became the Governor's Residence returned as guests. ◆

The lily pond adds its charm to the new Children's Garden. Landscape artist Kevin Norby designed the garden and Julie Kruse, horticulturist at the residence, directed the project and selected and planted the flowers. Private donations paid for the venture.

Menu

Buffet Lunch
for Ben Hummel's 5th Grade Class
April 21, 1993

Mostaccioli*

Cheese Toast

Chicken Fingers

Green Salad

Fruit Tray

Chocolate Chip Cookies

Milk

*Recipe follows

M ostaccioli

1   **pound ground beef**
¹/₂   **pound Italian sausage**
1   **large onion, diced**
1   **teaspoon minced garlic**
1   **can (28-ounce) tomato sauce**
¹/₂   **teaspoon basil**
¹/₂   **teaspoon thyme**
¹/₂   **teaspoon oregano**
1   **bay leaf**
     salt and pepper
10   **ounces mostaccioli (uncooked, about 3 cups)**
2-4   **tablespoons olive oil, as needed**
8   **ounces (2 cups) shredded mozzarella cheese**

In large skillet or Dutch oven, brown ground beef and Italian sausage; drain excess fat. Add onion and garlic; sauté until onion is limp but not brown. Stir in tomato sauce, herbs and bay leaf. Simmer 20 - 25 minutes, adding water if sauce is too thick. Add salt and pepper to taste. Meanwhile, place pasta in boiling water with a little olive oil. Cook until "al dente^" or desired doneness. Drain. Toss with a little olive oil. Place pasta on serving platter; top with sauce and mozzarella cheese.

6 to 8 servings

Variation: place pasta in a baking pan; top with sauce and cheese. Bake in a 350 degree oven for a few minutes to melt cheese.

^See tip on page 189

The chefs keep minced garlic in olive oil on hand at the Governor's Residence. It's available in jars at most local grocery stores. Or, use fresh garlic: 1 - 2 cloves equals approximately 1 teaspoon minced.

A summer garden party at the Governor's Residence

Events and very special guests

Minnesota's first families
have hosted
a dazzling array
of dignitaries and celebrities

The Carlsons enjoy hosting a variety of events. "Whether it is a Pulitzer prize winner, a fifth grade class, or a foreign dignitary, we want our guests to have a warm and pleasant experience," Susan says. "Both the governor and I make a point of personally greeting everyone at the front door. And, Jenny the schnauzer is also usually on hand to welcome guests."

Memorable events include sharing leftover chicken with Hillary Clinton in the kitchen, congratulatory receptions for the 1992 NIT Champion Minnesota Gopher basketball team and the St. Thomas women's basketball team after winning the 1991 NCAA Division III National Championship, and special parties

Dignitaries

With Governor Arne Carlson (far right) at a benefit held at the residence are former Minnesota governors (l. to r.) Orville Freeman, Elmer Andersen, Harold Stassen, Al Quie, and Wendell Anderson

Guests range from dignitaries to movie stars to school children

for children. "Long after leaving this place, I know I'll always remember our Easter Brunches where children faced with serious illnesses came to the Governor's Residence and just had fun," says Susan.

While mom and dad enjoy hosting their events, Jessica Carlson likes hosting movie stars. Her favorite guest was Arnold Schwarzenegger, because "he is a movie star from 'Kindergarten Cop' and I like his accent," Jessica says. Schwarzenegger lunched at the residence while in the Twin Cities representing the President's Council on Physical Fitness.

Early in their term, the Carlsons began holding "Community Leader" dinners with 12 to 14 guests. Education, business, religious and other community leaders spend an evening with the Carlsons talking about a wide range of subjects. "These dinners give Arne and me the opportunity to share ideas with people from all over Minnesota," Susan says.

Other Carlson guests include the former President from Costa Rica; ambassadors from France, Italy and Taiwan; Lamar Alexander, former Education Secretary under President George Bush; governors and first ladies from many states; famous actors; playwrights; sports stars; and one of the Carlsons' favorites — the Broadway

musical cast of "Joseph and the Amazing Technicolor Dreamcoat" with star Donny Osmond.

Fundraising has become a way of life for first families because most have used private, not public, funds for refurbishing and renovating the residence. "But fundraising can also be fun," says Susan. "One of our most memorable events was a major benefit celebrating the 80th birthday of the house." More than 300 people attended the black-tie gala plated dinner. Many were decked out in 1900s attire. Former Governor Wendell Anderson and Susan co-chaired the event.

A series of Artist Showcases featuring Minnesota artists and their work have continued to help raise funds for the residence. And a spring fashion extravaganza which the 1006 Summit Avenue Society sponsored at the residence drew more than 325 people in 1993.

Guests from around the world

While the Carlsons have entertained their share of celebrities and dignitaries, other first families also have impressive who's who guest lists.

Perhaps the most famous visitor to the residence was Soviet President Mikhail Gorbachev, who dined with the Perpich family in 1990. Gorbachev's trip to Minnesota to

The Needlework Guild of Minnesota stitched covers for dining room chairs as part of the 1976 bicentennial celebration. The state motto "L'Etoile du Nord" (The Star of the North) appears on each chair seat.

Royalty gets a taste of Minnesota hospitality and family life

meet with the nation's top business and agricultural leaders started with lunch at the residence. Gorbachev had expressed an interest in Minnesota author Sinclair Lewis, so Governor Perpich gave him an autographed first edition of *Main Street*. Lola Perpich gave Raisa Gorbachev a robe and gown by renowned Minnesota designer Valerie Fitzgerald.

The Quies celebrated "Scandinavia Today" in a more authentic way than most Minnesotans, hosting King Olav of Norway and King Carl Gustav and Queen Silvia of Sweden. Most Quie special guests, however, were regular citizens; the Quies held 27 drawings for Minnesotans to win a night at the residence.

The Andersons had one of the most varied visitor lists. In their four years at the residence, they hosted England's Princess Margaret, Supreme Court Chief Justice Warren Burger, Vice President Hubert Humphrey, Colonel Charles Lindberg, John Denver, Mary Tyler Moore, and Minnesota Senator Walter Mondale.

The country's bicentennial celebration prompted Mary Anderson to invite the Needlework Guild of Minnesota to make covers for the dining room chairs. To preserve the delicate work, the chairs are no longer used, but are on display to show off the handicraft of 36 stitchers.

Florence Rolvaag lamented to the *St. Paul Pioneer Press* that the residence did not have adequate guest rooms, but she managed to host an impressive list of dignitaries. Crown Prince Harald of Norway slept in Kristin Rolvaag's bedroom when he visited for the first official function in the residence.

The LeVanders also treated royalty to a slice of family life, entertaining French Ambassador Charles Lucet with an evening of French music on the phonograph. Other LeVander guests included England's Princess Alexandra and Lord Angus Ogilvy, Norway's King Olav V, and Joan and Senator Ted Kennedy ◆

First Lady Gretchen Quie and Governor Quie honor King Olav V of Norway (center) at a dinner in the Governor's Residence on October 7, 1982.

Server with hors d'oeuvres at the Gorbachev visit

Menu

Luncheon for
Soviet President Mikhail
and Raisa Gorbachev

June 3, 1990

Corncakes with Smoked Salmon, Crème Fraiche and Caviar
Pecan-Breaded Walleye with Artichokes, Smoked Tomatoes and Garden Greens*
Medallions of Provimi Veal with Morel Sauce
Wild Rice and Corn Compote*
Minted Sweet Biscuits Filled with Whipped Sweet and Sour Cream
Early Summer Berries and Caramel Sauce
Beaulieu Vineyard Carneros Chardonnay (1987)
Iron Horse Sonoma County Wedding Cuvée Blanc de Moirs (1987)

*Recipe follows

Pecan-Breaded Walleye
with Artichokes, Smoked Tomatoes and Garden Greens

1   tablespoon olive oil

3   tablespoons chopped sun-dried tomatoes

2   tablespoons chopped taggiasche olives

4   poached artichoke bottoms, chopped

1   tablespoon chopped basil

1   lemon

¹/₂   cup chopped roasted pecans

1   cup bread crumbs

4   pieces (3 ounces each) boneless, skinless walleye fillet

¹/₂   cup heavy cream

     salt

     vegetable oil

     baby mixed greens, washed (enough for 4 small salads)

¹/₂   cup vinaigrette dressing

¹/₂   cup *Nantais Butter****

¹/₂   cup smoked tomato purée

4   blue corn Madeleines or muffins

**See index for recipe

Preheat oven to 350 degrees. Sauté tomatoes, olives and artichokes in olive oil until heated through. Stir in basil and some juice from lemon; sauté lightly; remove from heat; keep warm. Combine pecans and bread crumbs; set aside. Moisten walleye in cream and season with salt; dredge in pecan-crumb mixture. Sauté walleye in small amount of vegetable oil until brown on both sides. Transfer fish to baking sheet; bake until fish flakes with a fork. Meanwhile, toss greens in vinaigrette and arrange in circles on plates. Combine *Nantais Butter* and smoked tomato purée; season with salt. Spoon sauce into center of greens. Set fish on sauce; garnish with artichoke mixture. Serve with blue corn Madeleines or muffins.

4 servings.

For smoked tomatoes, pureé 8 blanched red tomatoes (skins and seeds removed) in a blender. Place in a saucepan and bring to a boil. Add 1-2 tablespoons liquid smoke and salt and pepper to taste.

Wild Rice & Corn Compote

1¹/₂   cups cooked wild rice

¹/₄   cup diced ham

¹/₄   cup roasted corn kernels

¹/₄   cup blanched, hulled snap peas

2   tablespoons unsalted butter

2   tablespoons soy sauce

Combine all ingredients in large frying pan; sauté until heated through.

4 servings.

Anne Carlson Davis, her husband Andrew Davis, and their wedding party arrive at the residence following the ceremony.

Memorable weddings

"It was a special day
for all of us
— better than I could have imagined."

Anne Carlson Davis

When not hosting official visitors, 1006 Summit is like other homes along the avenue. And as in other homes, relatives and friends gather for life's special celebrations: birthdays, holidays, and weddings.

Friends and family gathered at 1006 Summit for the wedding reception of Jean LeVander and Thomas King, the first such happening at the Governor's Residence. The February 11, 1967, event followed shortly after Harold LeVander's inauguration and before the family had moved in.

"I went from working on the campaign to writing my father's speeches and didn't have time to plan my wedding," says Jean. "I became engaged in August,

Weddings

Jean LeVander King and Tom King cut their wedding cake in the solarium.

Food and festivities warm receptions on bitter cold nights

announced the engagement after the election, and got married in February. Mary Kelly organized the wedding after she finished being my dad's campaign manager."

A question of etiquette

Although she couldn't plan the wedding because of her tight schedule, Jean took time to cooperate with press coverage two weeks prior to it. As part of a Dayton's department store week-long bridal promotion, she and her mother, First Lady Iantha LeVander, moderated an informal question-and-answer session with etiquette authority Amy Vanderbilt. One question Jean asked was whether the groom should wear white gloves. Apparently Amy said yes, because not only the groom, but the bridesmaids, groomsmen, and parents of the couple were white-gloved for the wedding.

The candlelight ceremony took place at Gloria Dei Lutheran Church in St. Paul. The mothers of the bride and groom wore long formal gowns. All the men wore traditional white ties and tails.

"It was 32 degrees below zero the night we got married and everyone was huddled in the mansion," Jean says. "I remember it being very festive with a harpist playing on the balcony. But I don't remember the

food, because Tom and I were so busy visiting with our guests that we never got to eat. We stopped at Embers on Robert Street in West St. Paul after the reception."

Iantha, however, remembers what guests ate. She repeated the menu three years later for her son Hap's wedding reception. "For Jean, we planned a tea reception with Chicken Salad, Finger Sandwiches, and cookies served in the dining room, and punch and cake served in the solarium," Iantha says. "We did the same thing for Hap and Carla's wedding, November 15, 1969."

But the menu was not the only repeat. Like Jean and Tom, Hap and his bride, Carla Augst, had an 8 p.m. candlelight ceremony. The weather replayed a bitter cold night, and like Jean and Tom, the couple missed

Hap LeVander and Carla Augst LeVander cut their wedding cake in the dining room of the residence.

Rudy, Jr., Governor Perpich, First Lady Lola, and Mary Sue pose on the new terrace before guests arrive for Mary Sue's wedding reception.

"It was a magical September evening"

the food at the reception. "After greeting all the guests at church, we got in the car with Hap's best man and realized we were hungry," says Carla. "We stopped at a fast food place for a hamburger on the way to the reception. What we didn't realize was that the doors to the dining room were kept closed and nearly 300 guests waited for us to arrive before they could eat."

Carla says her memory of wedding reception details may have faded some but she clearly recalls the day she and Hap announced their engagement. "It was the end of July 1969, the day the astronauts landed on the moon," Carla says. "Hap and I went to the Governor's Residence for brunch. Because it was a state event, Hap waited until only a small group of friends remained at the front door to announce that we were engaged. Then we went to the garden, and as I sat on a rock, Hap knelt in front of me to show a friend with a camera how he had proposed. It was fun to see the rock again when I returned to the mansion for the dedication of the children's garden."

Fairy-tale wedding

Twenty years after Hap LeVander's wedding, Mary Sue Perpich, daughter of Governor Rudy and First Lady Lola Perpich, married Edward Bifulk on September 16, 1989, before 400 guests at the Basilica of St. Mary in Minneapolis. An introductory trumpet fanfare local celebrity Libby Larson had composed especially for the event resounded through the cathedral as the bride, hand on her father's arm, proceeded down the long aisle to where Archbishop Roach waited to preside.

Outside, a rented white Rolls Royce waited, ready to drive the couple away to the residence for a fairy-tale-like reception on the new brick terrace. "The reception at the mansion meant a lot, since we had lived there while the terrace renovation was being done," says Mary Sue. "It was a magical September evening. The gardens were beautiful, the moon was out, the fountain was flowing, the food was fabulous, and the cake was spectacular."

A harpist played as guests enjoyed an elegant buffet that included Pike Terrine with Sorrel Butter, Filo Tarts with

Colorful icing lilies adorn Mary Sue Perpich Bifulk and Edward Bifulk's wedding cake.

Anne Carlson Davis and Andrew Davis pose for a family photo with First Lady Susan, Anne's brother Tucker, Governor Arne Carlson, and Anne's sister Jessica.

Personal touches create warmth, elegance at Carlson wedding

Shrimp and Dill, and Strawberries Dipped in White Chocolate. An interesting aside came to light as the Perpich and Bifulk families got to know each other: Both the bride's and groom's fathers were dentists. And though the first lady used the nickname Lola, Delores was the given name of both mothers.

Magic lingers

Only four years after the Perpich wedding, Governor Arne Carlson and First Lady Susan announced the upcoming marriage of their daughter Anne to Andrew Davis. The couple had an afternoon ceremony with 10 bridesmaids and 10 groomsmen in attendance on April 24, 1993. Antique cars took the wedding party from Hennepin Avenue Methodist Church to an elegant reception at the residence where 350 guests and the music of the Larkspur Trio awaited their arrival.

The celebration took place under two heated tents beautifully decorated with an abundance of fresh tulips and candlelight. After a delicious buffet dinner, the live music of "Steve Millar and Diamondhead" moved the crowd from their chairs to an unforgettable evening of dancing on the terrace.

Anne wanted her reception to be light, fun, and enter-taining for friends and family. "You have to make all of your guests feel welcome and let them know that much of the joy of the event is sharing it with those you love," Anne says. "I wanted everyone to feel as though they left with something," So she gave her party personal touches.

Instead of standing in a receiving line, guests nibbled on almond and shrimp croquette appetizers, while Anne and Andrew walked among them and greeted each person. The wedding cakes were homemade creations of a 75-year-old Cambridge, Minnesota, woman. And Anne and Andrew out- of-town guests baskets filled with gifts such as wine and cheese, or crayons and notepads — whatever they felt would ap-peal to the receiver.

"My favorite thing about the wed-ding was being with friends and with my family, my husband, and my husband's family," Anne says. "It was a special day for all of us — better than I could have imagined. I wouldn't have done a thing differently." ◆

Anne Carlson chose an assortment of cakes, each of a different flavor.

*The Carlson wedding party
at the reception*

Menu

Wedding Reception for
Anne Carlson and Andrew Davis
April 24, 1993

Chicken in Puff Pastry with Port Wine Sauce*
Salmon Wellington with Nantais Butter**
Pommes Parisienne with Butter and Parsley
Broccoli and Cauliflower Flowerets with Red Pepper
Rice Pilaf
Assorted Cheese and Grapes
Assorted Breads
Italian Salad with Vinaigrette
Spinach Salad with Hot Bacon Dressing
Fruit Tray
Wedding Cake
*Recipe follows
**See index for recipe

Chicken in Puff Pastry *with Port Wine Sauce*

8	**chicken breasts (6 ounces each)**
	salt and pepper
1	**pint mushrooms, minced**
2	**tablespoons cream**
1	**egg yolk**
1	**tablespoon water**
8	**sheets puff pastry (about 4 inches square)**
	Port Wine Sauce

Preheat oven to 425 degrees. Season chicken with salt and pepper. Place on greased baking sheet. Bake 25 minutes; cool. To make duxelles, cook mushrooms in skillet (use little or no butter) until moisture is gone. Add cream; reduce until dry. Season to taste with salt and pepper; cool. Reduce oven temperature to 350 degrees. Slit chicken down center, three-fourths through. Stuff with 1 tablespoon duxelles. Beat egg yolk with 1 tablespoon water; brush pastry squares. Place chicken on pastry; pull gently on pastry to cover chicken, folding corners in envelope fashion. Turn upside down on greased baking sheet. Brush again with egg wash. Bake 15 - 20 minutes or until golden brown. Serve with *Port Wine Sauce*.

Serves 8.

Duxelles is a pre-prepared mixture of reduced mushrooms. It's used in this recipe as a stuffing. Don't thaw puff pastry too far ahead of time — it must be cold but not frozen to work with and it thaws quickly.

Port Wine Sauce

4	**cups ruby port wine**
2-3	**shallots, diced**
20	**black peppercorns**
1	**bay leaf**
1¼	**cups *Veal Stock*** or beef consommé**
4	**tablespoons roux^**
	salt and pepper

Combine wine, shallots, peppercorns and bay leaf in a saucepan. Cook over medium heat; reduce in volume by two-thirds. Add stock; reduce by one-third. Gradually stir in roux until sauce coats back of spoon. Season with salt and pepper. Strain through a fine sieve to remove shallots, peppercorns and bay leaf.

**See index for recipe
^See page 189 for tip

Menu

Wedding Reception for
Mary Sue Perpich and Edward Bifulk
September 16, 1989

Spinach Quiche

Small Tenderloin with Horseradish and French Bread

Pike Terrine with Sorrel Butter

Smoked Salmon with Capers, Onions, Eggs, Parsley, and French Bread

Boiled New Potatoes with Sour Cream and Caviar

Chicken and Leek Rolls   Filo Tarts with Shrimp and Dill*

Egg and Chive Pinwheels   Broiled Ham and Cheese on Croutons

Cheese and Green Onion on Toast Rounds

Cucumber Hearts with Salmon Mousse

Herb Cheese Heart Toast   Sausage with Puff Pastry*

Grilled Swordfish with Béarnaise Sauce

Shrimp and Snow Peas

Fruit Tray

Strawberries with Stems, Dipped in White Chocolate

Lemon Bars   Brownies   Wedding Cake

*Recipe follows

Filo Tarts with Shrimp and Dill

4	tablespoons butter
¹/₂	pound cooked salad shrimp
¹/₄	cup fresh chopped dill
	salt and pepper
6	filo sheets (12 inches x 18 inches)

Melt 2 tablespoons butter in sauté pan; add shrimp and dill. Season with salt and pepper to taste. Chill mixture. Preheat oven to 375 degrees. Melt remaining 2 tablespoons butter. Spread filo sheets with melted butter; lay one on top of the other. Cut into six 3-inch strips. Divide filling evenly on each strip; fold into triangles (flag fashion). Brush with butter. Bake 15 to 20 minutes.

6 servings.

Sausage in Puff Pastry

2	sheets puff pastry (about 4 inches square)
1	pound Polska Kielbasa sausage, cooked (one link)
1	egg yolk
2	tablespoons heavy cream

Lay puff pastry sheets end-to-end and seal with ice water. Place sausage link in center of dough. Fold short edges in; roll lengthwise to encase sausage. Seal with ice water and place on a baking sheet, seam-side down. Chill 30 minutes; remove from refrigerator. Preheat oven to 400 degrees. Combine egg yolk with cream; brush over pastry. Score top of pastry. Bake 25 to 30 minutes. Cut into 16 one-inch slices and serve warm with your favorite mustard.

8 to 10 servings.

Menu

Wedding Receptions for
Jean LeVander and Thomas R. King

February 11, 1967

and

Carla Augst and Harold P. "Hap" LeVander

November 15, 1969

Chicken Salad*

Finger Sandwiches

Mixed Nuts

Cookies

Bridal Cake

Champagne

Fruit Punch*

*Recipe follows

Chicken Salad

2   cups sour cream
1   cup mayonnaise
$^1/_2$ teaspoon dry mustard
2   teaspoons lemon juice
2   tablespoons horseradish
    dash of cayenne pepper
    salt to taste
6   cups cooked chicken pieces
$2^1/_2$ cups diced celery
6   tablespoons sweet pickles,
    minced
$1^1/_2$ cups salted slivered almonds,
    toasted
    hard-boiled eggs
    tomato slices

Combine first 7 ingredients; blend well and chill. Combine chicken, celery, sweet pickles and almonds. Stir in chilled dressing mixture. Toss until thoroughly mixed; chill. Remove from refrigerator; garnish with hard-boiled eggs and tomato slices.

12 servings.

Fruit Punch

$1^1/_2$ cups sugar
1   quart strong hot tea
1   quart orange juice
1   cup lemon juice
1   quart ginger ale
    fresh mint leaves
    large block of ice

Dissolve sugar in hot tea; mix with citrus juices. Pour over large block of ice. Before serving, add ginger ale; garnish with fresh mint.

Approximately 24 servings.

Variation: Add fresh fruits such as strawberries, shredded pineapple, or sliced peaches to the bowl; or use $^1/_2$ cup fruit syrup instead of sugar.

Chef Kenneth Grogg in the kitchen

Chef Nathan Cardarelle puts
finishing touches on a buffet table.

188

Al Dente: " to the tooth." The pasta should be cooked just enough to retain a somewhat firm texture.

Blanch: To plunge vegetables or seafood into boiling water for only a few seconds and then plunge into cold water to stop the cooking process.

Braise: To cook foods slowly and covered, in very little liquid.

Deglaze: Adding wine, water or stock to pan over high heat, removing the bits of browned food remaining in the pan. This adds a rich flavor to the sauce or dish.

Dredge: To lightly coat food with flour, bread crumbs, or cornmeal before sautéing or baking.

Reduce: To reduce the volume of liquid in a stock or sauce by boiling at medium heat. Reduction intensifies the flavors of the ingredients in the liquid.

Roux: A thickening ingredient used in sauces, gravies and some soups. It is usually made from equal parts of melted butter (or oil) and flour. White roux is most often used in recipes in this book. Sometime recipes may call for brown roux. This roux uses the same ingredients and measurements but has been browned over low heat to give a nuttier taste.

Sauté: The French term for browning food quickly in hot oil or butter.

Seasoned flour: Used to lightly bread meat or fish before sautéing. It consists of flour, salt, pepper and/or your favorite herbs.

Seasoned pan: A pan that has been treated to keep foods from sticking. To season a pan: First heat the dry pan until hot, then add vegetable oil and heat until almost smoking; remove the oil and coat with salt, rub carefully with a dry towel; discard salt. Cool pan and lightly rub with oil. From time to time, you should reseason pans. Always heat your pan, even nonstick pans, first before adding oil for cooking. If the pan and oil are hot, foods won't stick or absorb too much oil.

Skim: To remove fat from stocks or sauces with a spoon or ladle.

Kitchen Talk

Nutritional information

First Lady Susan Carlson enjoys a meal in the kitchen's dining nook.

In the information age of the '90s, our cookbook should provide readers with nutritional information. It allows you to plan your dietary needs and still enjoy fine foods in moderation. Whether you are counting calories or fat grams to lose weight or just trying to make calories count toward good nutrition, be sure to look at the following nutritional analysis.

Nutrient figures given are based on the following assumptions:

◆ When a range is given for an ingredient (3 to 3$^{1}/_{2}$ cups of flour), the lesser amount is calculated.

◆ When a range is given for a recipe yield, the greater amount is calculated.

◆ Optional ingredients, such as garnishes, are not calculated.

◆ The nutritional analysis of those recipes containing meat was calculated after all fat was removed.

◆ When the amount of salt is not listed, $^{3}/_{4}$ teaspoon is calculated.

◆ All butter and broth used in these recipes is unsalted. Canned products listed in the recipes contain salt. Those wishing to reduce their sodium intake should use salt-free versions of the listed ingredients.

I used the computer software program, *Santé,* a product of Hopkins Technology, a Minnesota company, to determine nutritional values.

Susan Carlson

Al's Best Doggone Pancakes
Per serving (based on 9 pancakes per recipe):
91 calories; 3 g protein; 3 g fat; 13 g carbohydrates;
432 mg sodium; 34 mg cholesterol.

Anadama Bread
Per serving (based on 12 slices per loaf):
110 calories; 2 g protein; 1 g fat; 24 g carbohydrates;
179 mg sodium; 1 mg cholesterol.

Apple Cake
Per serving (based on 9 slices per loaf):
271 calories; 3 g protein; 11 g fat; 41 g
carbohydrates;
76 mg sodium; 29 mg cholesterol.

Apple Strudel
Per serving (based on 10 slices per recipe):
437 calories; 5 g protein; 14 g fat; 74 g
carbohydrates;
175 mg sodium; 24 mg cholesterol.

Arne's Hot Chili
Per serving (based on 12 servings per recipe):
404 calories; 28 g protein; 17 g fat; 36 g
carbohydrates;
1677 mg sodium; 74 mg cholesterol.

Arne's Swedish Pancakes
Per serving (based on 6 pancakes per recipe):
121 calories; 3 g protein; 8 g fat; 10 g carbohydrates;
69 mg sodium; 106 mg cholesterol.

Aurore Sauce
Per Serving (based on 8 servings per recipe):
78 calories; trace protein; 8 g fat; 2 g carbohydrates;
160 mg sodium; 5 mg cholesterol.

Baked Salmon
Per 4 oz. serving:
417 calories; 23 g protein; 35 g fat; 1 g
carbohydrates;
700 mg sodium; 120 mg cholesterol.

Beer Batter Pan Fish
Per 5 oz. serving (walleye pike used for nutritional analysis):
373 calories; 33 g protein; 7 g fat; 36 g
carbohydrates;
586 mg sodium; 78 mg cholesterol.

Black Bean Soup
Per serving:
62 calories; 4 g protein; 1 g fat; 10 g carbohydrates;
307 mg sodium; 21 mg cholesterol.

Blitzen Torte
Per serving:
382 calories; 5 g protein; 20 g fat; 49 g
carbohydrates;
62 mg sodium; 136 mg cholesterol.

Braised Vegetables
Per serving:
124 calories; 6 g protein; 2 g fat; 22 g carbohydrates;
214 mg sodium; 1 mg cholesterol.

Brandy Snaps
Per cookie (based on 6 dozen cookies per recipe):
72 calories; trace protein; 3 g fat; 11 g carbohydrates;
5 mg sodium; 7 mg cholesterol.

Breakfast Toquitos
Per serving (based on using 1 tsp picante sauce per toquito):
338 calories; 24 g protein; 18 g fat; 21 g
carbohydrates;
782 mg sodium; 268 mg cholesterol.

Breast of Pheasant/Cream Gravy
Per 8 oz. serving:
1223 calories; 86 g protein; 81 g fat; 36 g
carbohydrates;
762 mg sodium; 361 mg cholesterol.

Broccoli with Browned Butter
Per serving:
103 calories; 2 g protein; 10 g fat; 4 g carbohydrates;
11 mg sodium; 24 mg cholesterol.

Brown Veal Stock
Nutritional information not included.

Cajun Blue Cheese Potatoes
Per serving:
242 calories; 7 g protein; 11 g fat; 31 g
carbohydrates;
463 mg sodium; 18 mg cholesterol.

Carrot Pudding
Per serving:
725 calories; 9 g protein; 48 g fat; 73 g
carbohydrates;
393 mg sodium; 111 mg cholesterol.

Cheese Rarebit
Per serving:
403 calories; 22 g protein; 26 g fat; 17 g
carbohydrates;
625 mg sodium; 79 mg cholesterol.

Cheese Souffle
Per serving:
472 calories; 23 g protein; 38 g fat; 10 g
carbohydrates;
580 mg sodium; 371 mg cholesterol.

Cheese Sticks
Per stick (based on using 4 tbls parmesan cheese):
32 calories; 1 g protein; 2 g fat; 2 g carbohydrates;
65 mg sodium; 7 mg cholesterol.

Chestnut Stuffing
Per serving (based on 12 servings per recipe):
222 calories; 12 g protein; 7 g fat; 24 g
carbohydrates;
644 mg sodium; 24 mg cholesterol.

Chicken Breast Fromage
Per 4 oz. serving:
516 calories; 44 g protein; 32 g fat; 8 g
carbohydrates;
579 mg sodium; 172 mg cholesterol.

Chicken Chasseur
Per 4 oz. serving:
330 calories; 29 g protein; 18 g fat; 7 g
carbohydrates;
98 mg sodium; 107 mg cholesterol.

Chicken in Puff Pastry
Per 6 oz. serving:
366 calories; 42 g protein; 15 g fat; 12 g
carbohydrates;
183 mg sodium; 131 mg cholesterol.

Chicken Gretchen's Way
Per 4 oz. serving:
584 calories; 33 g protein; 43 g fat; 17 g
carbohydrates;
519 mg sodium; 131 mg cholesterol.

Chicken Salad
Per serving (based on using 2 oz. chicken per serving,
using 3 eggs and 3 tomatoes):
403 calories; 20 g protein; 32 g fat; 10 g
carbohydrates;
394 mg sodium; 111 mg cholesterol.

Chicken Veronique
Per 4 oz. serving:
428 calories; 31 g protein; 23 g fat; 18 g
carbohydrates;
379 mg sodium; 128 mg cholesterol.

Chilled Papaya Bisque
Per serving (based on 8 servings per recipe):
193 calories; 2 g protein; 7 g fat; 25 g carbohydrates;
160 mg sodium; 22 mg cholesterol.

Chocolate-Orange Sauce
Per serving:
604 calories; 1 g protein; 17 g fat; 100 g
carbohydrates;
27 mg sodium; 24 mg cholesterol.

Chocolate Sauce
Per 1/4 cup serving:
202 calories; 1 g protein; 13 g fat; 23 g
carbohydrates;
17 mg sodium; 32 mg cholesterol.

Cipolle's Spaghetti Sauce
Per 1/2 cup serving:
170 calories; 2 g protein; 14 g fat; 10 g
carbohydrates;
234 mg sodium; 0 cholesterol.

Cold Raspberry Souffle
Per serving:
137 calories; 3 g protein; 3 g fat; 26 g carbohydrates;
185 mg sodium; 5 mg cholesterol.

Coq au Vin
Per 4 oz. serving:
309 calories; 34 g protein; 13 g fat; 8 g
carbohydrates;
332 mg sodium; 85 mg cholesterol.

Corn Bread Stuffing
Per serving (based on 12 servings per recipe):
347 calories; 11 g protein; 13 g fat; 48 g
carbohydrates;
912 mg sodium; 48 mg cholesterol.

Court Bouillon
Nutritional information not included.

Creamed Herb Pheasant
Per 8 oz. serving:
722 calories; 76 g protein; 40 g fat; 11 g
carbohydrates;
350 mg sodium; 237 mg cholesterol.

Creme Anglaise
Per serving (based on 8 servings per recipe):
314 calories; 8 g protein; 12 g fat; 43 g
carbohydrates;
73 mg sodium; 343 mg cholesterol.

Crepes Elaine
Includes: Dessert Crepes & Chocolate-Orange Sauce
Per serving (based on using 2 oz. ice cream per crepe):
1112 calories; 14 g protein; 43 g fat; 155 g
carbohydrates;
216 mg sodium; 176 mg cholesterol.

Crown Roast of Pork
Per 7 oz. serving:
771 calories; 56 g protein; 58 g fat; 2 g
carbohydrates;
717 mg sodium; 229 mg cholesterol.

Cucumber Salad
Per serving:
152 calories; 1 g protein; 11 g fat; 15 g
carbohydrates;
2988 mg sodium; 0 cholesterol.

Curried Chicken Salad
Per serving (based on 10 - 2 1/2 oz. of chicken per serving):
517 calories; 25 g protein; 41 g fat; 14 g
carbohydrates;
588 mg sodium; 126 mg cholesterol.

Eggs Shepard
Per serving:
142 calories; 9 g protein; 7 g fat; 13 g carbohydrates;
291 mg sodium; 212 mg cholesterol.

Fettucini Carbonara
Per serving:
621 calories; 23 g protein; 35 g fat; 50 g
carbohydrates;
820 mg sodium; 196 mg cholesterol.

Filet Gorgonzola
Per 6 oz. serving:
524 calories; 58 g protein; 28 g fat; 1 g
carbohydrates;
685 mg sodium; 167 mg cholesterol.

Fillet of Walleye Pike Almandine
Per 1/3 lbs serving (based on using 8 oz. melted butter,
4 oz. bread crumbs and 4 oz. almonds):
487 calories; 34 g protein; 33 g fat; 11 g
carbohydrates;
357 mg sodium; 143 mg cholesterol.

Continued

191

Fillo Tarts/Shrimp & Dill
Per serving:
171 calories; 11 g protein; 10 g fat; 10 g carbohydrates;
388 mg sodium; 77 mg cholesterol.

Flourless Chocolate Torte
Per serving (based on 8 servings per recipe):
535 calories; 6 g protein; 40 g fat; 47 g carbohydrates;
44 mg sodium; 231 mg cholesterol.

French Onion Soup/Carlson's
Per serving (based on 8 servings and using low fat swiss cheese):
315 calories; 14 g protein; 18 g fat; 24 g carbohydrates; 1013 mg sodium; 53 mg cholesterol.

French Onion Soup/Anderson's
Per serving (based on 6 servings):
431 calories; 22 g protein; 26 g fat; 26 g carbohydrates; 1102 mg sodium; 115 mg cholesterol.

Fruit Dressing
Per 1/2 cup serving:
139 calories; 3 g protein; 5 g fat; 21 g carbohydrates;
144 mg sodium; 5 mg cholesterol.

Fruit Punch
Per 8 - 3/4 oz. serving:
162 calories; 1 g protein; trace fat; 41 g carbohydrates; 11 mg sodium; 0 cholesterol.

German Oven Pancake
Per serving (based on using 2 oz. powdered sugar and 4 tbls melted butter):
270 calories; 7 g protein; 15 g fat; 27 g carbohydrates; 200 mg sodium; 235 mg cholesterol.

Gingered Chicken Broth
Per serving (based on 4 servings per recipe):
32 calories; 1.55 g protein; 2 g fat; 1 g carbohydrates;
234 mg sodium; 2 mg cholesterol.

Glazed Berries in Syrup
Per serving (based on using 8 pecan lace cups per recipe):
222 calories; trace protein; trace fat; 57 g carbohydrates; 2 mg sodium; 0 cholesterol.

Glazed Fresh Trout
Per serving (based on 5 main course servings per recipe):
936 calories; 63 g protein; 69 g fat; 3 g carbohydrates; 957 mg sodium; 195 mg cholesterol.

Glazed Fresh Trout
Per serving (based on 10 first course servings per recipe):
390 calories; 26 g protein; 29 g fat; 1 g carbohydrates;
399 mg sodium; 81 mg cholesterol.

Grand Marnier Souffle
Per serving:
173 calories; 7 g protein; 4 g fat; 23 g carbohydrates;
84 mg sodium; 90 mg cholesterol.

Grandma Quie's Coconut Bars
Per bar (based on 2 1/2 dozen bars per recipe):
134 calories; 2 g protein; 7 g fat; 17 g carbohydrates;
40 mg sodium; 26 mg cholesterol.

Grandma Shepard's Cookies
Per cookie (based on 9 dozen cookies per recipe):
49 calories; 1 g protein; 2 g fat; 8 g carbohydrates;
6 mg sodium; 6 mg cholesterol.

Granny Irvine's Fudge Bars
Per serving:
164 calories; 2 g protein; 12 g fat; 14 g carbohydrates;
131 mg sodium; 74 mg cholesterol.

Green and White Chicken
Per 4 oz. serving (based on using 6 tbls romano cheese):
845 calories; 34 g protein; 56 g fat; 51 g carbohydrates;
1083 mg sodium; 204 mg cholesterol.

Ham Glaze a la Carlson
Per 6 - 1/4 oz. serving (includes ham):
435 calories; 41 g protein; 17 g fat; 26 g carbohydrates;
1801 mg sodium; 111 mg cholesterol.

Hot Cracker Topper
Per serving:
265 calories; 5 g protein; 26 g fat; 5 g carbohydrates;
403 mg sodium; 39 mg cholesterol.

Klub
Per serving (based on using 10 dumplings from recipe and
10 tsp melted butter):
275 calories; 5 g protein; 13 g fat; 34 g carbohydrates;
407 mg sodium; 20 mg cholesterol.

Kottbullar
Per serving:
366 calories; 22 g protein; 19 g fat; 25 g carbohydrates;
731 mg sodium; 113 mg cholesterol.

Lamb and Cabbage
Per serving:
381 calories; 46 g protein; 12 g fat; 22 g carbohydrates;
411 mg sodium; 142 mg cholesterol.

Lamb Pebronetta
Per serving:
281 calories; 22 g protein; 19 g fat; 4 g carbohydrates;
290 mg sodium; 77 mg cholesterol.

Lobster Salad
Per serving (based on 8 servings and using 4 oz. lobster
per serving):
366 calories; 28 g protein; 23 g fat; 14 g carbohydrates;
326 mg sodium; 298 mg cholesterol.

Lobster Thermidor
Per serving (based on 7 oz. lobster per serving and 8 tbls parmesan cheese):
622 calories; 40 g protein; 43 g fat; 13 g carbohydrates;
1049 mg sodium; 379 mg cholesterol.

Marilyn's Hot German Potato Salad
Per serving:
213 calories; 4 g protein; 15 g fat; 18 g carbohydrates;
429 mg sodium; 28 mg cholesterol.

Marinated Green Beans
Per serving:
294 calories; 3 g protein; 27 g fat; 12 g carbohydrates;
282 mg sodium; 0 cholesterol.

Minnesota Wild Rice
Per serving:
250 calories; 5 g protein; 16 g fat; 23 g carbohydrates;
358 mg sodium; 40 mg cholesterol.

Mint Sauce
Per cup:
99 calories; 0 protein; 0 fat; 28 g carbohydrates;
1 mg sodium; 0 cholesterol.

Mostaccioli
Per serving:
529 calories; 32 g protein; 29 g fat; 15 g carbohydrates;
1138 mg sodium; 129 mg cholesterol.

Mrs. Anderson's Casserole
Per serving:
384 calories; 36 g protein; 18 g fat; 17 g carbohydrates;
1294 mg sodium; 137 mg cholesterol.

Mushroom Croustades
Per serving (based on using 3 tbls parmesan cheese):
157 calories; 3 g protein; 10 g fat; 15 g carbohydrates;
211 mg sodium; 24 mg cholesterol.

Mustard Sauce/Carlson's
Per 1/3 cup serving:
161 calories; 2 g protein; 7 g fat; 5 g carbohydrates;
192 mg sodium; 18 mg cholesterol.

Mustard Sauce/Irvine's
Per 1/3 cup serving:
243 calories; 3 g protein; 19 g fat; 18 g carbohydrates;
139 mg sodium; 107 mg cholesterol.

Nantais Butter
Per 1/4 cup serving:
531 calories; 1 g protein; 49 g fat; 2 g carbohydrates;
235 mg sodium; 134 mg cholesterol.

Norwegian Meatballs & Gravy
Per serving:
445 calories; 32 g protein; 27 g fat; 16 g carbohydrates;
481 mg sodium; 184 mg cholesterol.

Orange Honey Dressing
Per serving (based on 10 servings per recipe):
202 calories; trace protein; 18 g fat; 11 g carbohydrates;
232 mg sodium; 0 cholesterol.

Daisy and Jenny waiting for treats

Oyster Bisque
Per serving:
635 calories; 11 g protein; 61 g fat; 13 g carbohydrates;
388 mg sodium; 241 mg cholesterol.

Pastry Cream
Per 1/4 cup serving:
132 calories; 3 g protein; 4 g fat; 19 g carbohydrates;
33 mg sodium; 90 mg cholesterol.

Pecan-Breaded Walleye
Per serving:
1082 calories; 29 g protein; 75 g fat; 50 g
carbohydrates;
1699 mg sodium; 222 mg cholesterol.

Pecan Lace Cups
Includes: Glazed Berries
Per serving (based on using 4 oz. ice milk):
727 calories; 4 g protein; 29 g fat; 119 g carbohydrates;
332 mg sodium; 50 mg cholesterol.

Pecan Pie
Per serving (based on 6 servings per recipe):
977 calories; 10 g protein; 48 g fat; 133 g
carbohydrates;
836 mg sodium; 250 mg cholesterol.

Pepper Steak
Per 6 oz. serving:
474 calories; 50 g protein; 25 g fat; 2 g carbohydrates;
160 mg sodium; 159 mg cholesterol.

Pineapple Split
Per serving:
491 calories; 4 g protein; 33 g fat; 46 g carbohydrates;
171 mg sodium; 59 mg cholesterol.

Pineapple Turkey Salad
Per serving (based on 3 oz. turkey per serving
and using 1 cup mayonnaise):
327 calories; 13 g protein; 28 g fat; 9 g carbohydrates;
989 mg sodium; 36 mg cholesterol.

Poached Pears in Port Wine
Per serving:
254 calories; 1 g protein; 1 g fat; 51 g carbohydrates;
6 mg sodium; 0 cholesterol.

Pommes Croquettes
Per serving (based on 8 servings and using 1 tbls oil):
559 calories; 19 g protein; 15 g fat; 75 g carbohydrates;
656 mg sodium; 266 mg cholesterol.

Pommes Dauphinoise
Per serving:
281 calories; 7 g protein; 19 g fat; 22 g
carbohydrates;
236 mg sodium; 67 mg cholesterol.

Pork Tenderloin W/Mustard Sauce
Per 4 oz. serving:
305 calories; 26 g protein; 10 g fat; 7 g
carbohydrates;
252 mg sodium; 84 mg cholesterol.

Port Wine Sauce
Per serving (based on 8 servings per recipe):
168 calories; 2 g protein; 7 g fat; 7 g carbohydrates;
20 mg sodium; 16 mg cholesterol.

Raspberry Coulis
Per serving (based on 8 servings per recipe):
119 calories; trace protein; trace fat; 30
carbohydrates;
trace sodium; 0 cholesterol.

Red Cabbage
Per serving:
73 calories; 1 g protein; 2 g fat; 13 g carbohydrates;
192 mg sodium; 2 mg cholesterol.

Red Wine Sauce
Per 1 1/3 oz. serving:
40 calories; trace protein; trace fat; 9 g
carbohydrates;
38 mg sodium; 0 cholesterol.

Remoulade Sauce
Served with Glazed Fresh Trout
Per serving (based on 5 servings per recipe):
321 calories; 1 g protein; 35 g fat; trace
carbohydrates;
346 mg sodium; 19 mg cholesterol.

Remoulade Sauce
Served with Glazed Fresh Trout
Per serving (based on 10 servings):
162 calories; trace protein; 18 g fat; 1 g
carbohydrates;
333 mg sodium; 10 mg cholesterol.

Rouladen
Per serving (based on 8 tsp dijon mustard,
1/2 cup flour and 4 tbls butter):
383 calories; 45 g protein; 18 g fat; 8 g
carbohydrates;
1144 mg sodium; 132 mg cholesterol.

Ruth's Cheesecake
Per serving:
392 calories; 7 g protein; 29 g fat; 28 g
carbohydrates;
207 mg sodium; 179 mg cholesterol.

Saffron Rice
Per serving (based on 8 servings per recipe):
235 calories; 5 g protein; 5 g fat; 40 g carbohydrates;
38 mg sodium; 10 mg cholesterol.

Sarma
Per serving (based on 22 sarmas and using
6 bacon strips):
174 calories; 15 g protein; 7 g fat; 12 g
carbohydrates;
837 mg sodium; 52 mg cholesterol.

Sauerbraten
Per serving:
554 calories; 51 g protein; 29 g fat; 18 g
carbohydrates;
979 mg sodium; 160 mg cholesterol.

Sausage in Puff Pastry
Per serving:
268 calories; 9 g protein; 23 g fat; 6 g carbohydrates;
646 mg sodium; 70 mg cholesterol.

Scallop Ragout
Per serving:
440 calories; 28 g protein; 29 g fat; 10 g
carbohydrates;
457 mg sodium; 135 mg cholesterol.

Seafood Pasta Alfredo
Per serving:
534 calories; 31 g protein; 33 g fat; 28 g
carbohydrates;
1026 mg sodium; 211 mg cholesterol.

Shrimp Creole
Per serving:
284 calories; 17 g protein; 8 g fat; 35 g
carbohydrates;
553 mg sodium; 113 mg cholesterol.

Shrimp Salad Macadamia
Per serving (based on using 40 oz. shrimp):
455 calories; 28 g protein; 35 g fat; 8 g
carbohydrates;
501 mg sodium; 213 mg cholesterol.

Spinach and Bacon Salad
Per serving:
300 calories; 8 g protein; 28 g fat; 8 g carbohydrates;
614 mg sodium; 42 mg cholesterol.

Spinach-Filled Tomatoes
Per serving:
351 calories; 15 g protein; 27 g fat; 14 g carbohydrates;
947 mg sodium; 67 mg cholesterol.

Spinach Wild Rice Salad
Per serving:
183 calories; 7 g protein; 11 g fat; 15 g
carbohydrates;
343 mg sodium; 10 mg cholesterol.

Strawberry Ice Cream
Per serving (based on using 3/4 cup sugar):
276 calories; 2 g protein; 24 g fat; 16 g
carbohydrates;
96 mg sodium; 87 mg cholesterol.

Summit Cheese Ball
Per serving:
168 calories; 5 g protein; 16 g fat; 3 g carbohydrates;
260 mg sodium; 40 mg cholesterol.

Susan's Meat Loaf
Per serving (based on 6 servings per recipe):
461 calories; 38 g protein; 23 g fat; 20 g
carbohydrates;
1093 mg sodium; 169 mg cholesterol.

Swedish Rye Bread
Per slice (based on 6 slices per loaf):
276 calories; 7 g protein; 4 g fat; 55 g carbohydrates;
195 mg sodium; 4 mg cholesterol.

Tomato Aspic
Per serving:
81 calories; 3 g protein; 1 g fat; 17 g carbohydrates;
443 mg sodium; 0 cholesterol.

Veal Birds
Per serving (based on using 2 tbls flour):
427 calories; 45 g protein; 19 g fat; 15 g
carbohydrates;
577 mg sodium; 250 mg cholesterol.

Veal Marsala
Per 6 oz. serving:
367 calories; 38 g protein; 19 g fat; 3 g
carbohydrates;
716 mg sodium; 134 mg cholesterol.

Veal Piccata
Per 4 oz. serving:
562 calories; 29 g protein; 36 g fat; 30 g
carbohydrates;
262 mg sodium; 194 mg cholesterol.

Vegetable Strata
Per serving:
350 calories; 17 g protein; 19 g fat; 28 g
carbohydrates;
648 mg sodium; 297 mg cholesterol.

Venison Forestiere
Per 6 oz. serving:
384 calories; 38 g protein; 12 g fat; 13 g
carbohydrates;
487 mg sodium; 106 mg cholesterol.

Venison Stock
Nutritional information not included.

Vichyssoise
Per serving:
280 calories; 5 g protein; 19 g fat; 23 g
carbohydrates;
367 mg sodium; 55 mg cholesterol.

Watermelon Pickles
Per pint:
873 calories; 7 g protein; trace fat; 221 g
carbohydrates;
9381 mg sodium; 0 cholesterol.

West Coast Salad
Per serving (based on 8 servings per recipe):
224 calories; 3 g protein; 19 g fat; 11 g
carbohydrates;
298 mg sodium; 0 cholesterol.

Whole Lobster
Nutritional information not included.

Wild Rice & Corn Compote
Per serving (based on 4 servings per recipe):
185 calories; 5 g protein; 9 g fat; 21 g carbohydrates;
1131 mg sodium; 34 mg cholesterol.

Wild Rice Pilaf
Per serving:
238 calories; 6 g protein; 11 g fat; 32 g
carbohydrates;
459 mg sodium; 20 mg cholesterol.

Wild Rice Soup
Per serving:
371 calories; 5 g protein; 33 g fat; 14 g
carbohydrates;
626 mg sodium; 100 mg cholesterol. ◆

Menu Index

An early morning breakfast meeting on the porch at The Governor's Residence

Recipe Index

Continued

Recipe index, cont.

Mother Nature helped Minnesota celebrate the Twins winning the World Series with the "storm of the century" on Halloween night 1991.

The Governor's Residence extends good wishes to the University of Minnesota Golden Gophers.

𝒫hotograph 𝒥ndex

Acknowledgments

Executive Editor
Susan Shepard Carlson

Editor/Cookbook Committee Chair
Jean Steiner

Design and Desktop Publishing
Barbara Ladd

Editing Assistance
Trish Grafstrom and Jennifer Messenger

Contributing Writers
Susan Carlson: *Nutritional Information and Anaylsis*
Connie Carrino: *The '70s, Cooking Tips,* and *Kitchen Talk*
Jean Goad: *A Look Back at the Early Years* and *Celebrations/Especially for Children*
Trish Grafstrom: *The '80s* and *Celebrations/Memorable Weddings*
Teresa A. Hudoba: *The '60s* and *Celebrations/Children's Garden*
Jennifer Messenger: *Celebrations/Events and Very Special Guests*
Jean Steiner: *Contents, Preface, Introduction, The '90s*

Recipe and Cooking Tips provided by
Chefs Nathan Cardarelle and Kenneth Grogg, *The '80s* and *The '90s*
Ruth Knutson, *The '60s, The '70s,* and *The '80s*

Recipe Coordination
Connie Carrino, Teresa A. Hudoba, Shiela Oien

Recipe Committee and Testers
Erma Andrews, Jean Beattie, Connie Carrino, Laura Kaumann, Jean Goad, Barb Halbakken, Peggy Henniger,
Pat Johnson, Kathy Kingman, Betty Norgaard, Betsy Norum, Jean Trosdahl

Indexing
Teresa A. Hudoba

Marketing/Sales/Operations
Dee Arnold Wilkie, Chair
Marge Gasch, Barb Halbakken, Dolly Hickman, Barbara Hoffmann, Kathy Kingman, Barbara Shaw Nelson,
Joan O'Brien, Alison O'Connell, Shiela Oien, Lois Schlampp, Sharon Sorenson

Public Relations
Mary Ann DeRosier and Michelle Albers

Budget and Finance
Deb Frenzel, President, 1006 Summit Avenue Society
Florence McCarthy, Treasurer, 1006 Summit Avenue Society

Contributing Photographers
Peter Beck, Len Dixon, Frank Mikacevich, Carleton Rust, and Don Waldhauser

Technical Assistance
Shiela Oien

Residence and Executive Editor Assistance
Barbara Hoffmann, Residence Director; Michelle Albers, Public Relations Assistant; Joyce Pellow, Administrative Assistant

Special Thanks
First Families; Olivia Irvine Dodge;
The 1006 Summit Avenue Society Board and Members; and Betsy Norum for her continued dedication to this project